Sussex

Edited By Megan Roberts

First published in Great Britain in 2019 by:

Young Writers
Remus House
Coltsfoot Drive
Peterborough
PE2 9BF
Telephone: 01733 890066
Website: www.youngwriters.co.uk

FOREWORD

Here at Young Writers, we love to let imaginations run wild and creativity go crazy. Our aim is to encourage young people to get their creative juices flowing and put pen to paper. Each competition is tailored to the relevant age group, hopefully giving each pupil the inspiration and incentive to create their own piece of creative writing, whether it's a poem or a short story. By allowing them to see their own work in print, we know their confidence and love for the written word will grow.

For our latest competition Poetry Wonderland, we invited primary school pupils to create wild and wonderful poems on any topic they liked – the only limits were the limits of their imagination! Using poetry as their magic wand, these young poets have conjured up worlds, creatures and situations that will amaze and astound or scare and startle! Using a variety of poetic forms of their own choosing, they have allowed us to get a glimpse into their vivid imaginations. We hope you enjoy wandering through the wonders of this book as much as we have.

★ CONTENTS ★

Arun Webb (10)	68
Natalie Kiara Kocaiova (10)	69
Abigail Lish (10)	70
Amy Carrigan (9)	71
Thea Stott (10)	72
Anoushka Millie Musgrave (11)	73
Iestyn James (10)	74
Zach Jude Whittingham (10)	75
Grace Wells (10)	76
Ellie Wright (9)	77
Amelie Bourne (10)	78
Maisy Standing (9)	79
Harry Luke Kinsey (10)	80
Yara Penfold (10)	81
Max Weightman-Achille (9)	82
Sophie Rose Biggs (10)	83
Harry Langley (10)	84
Jacob Doorly (9)	85
Jake Cotton-Hewitt (10)	86
Lili Angus (10)	87
Finley C (9)	88
Emma Harrison (9)	89
Violette Paul (9) & Dixie Probyn	90
Casper Davenport (9)	91
Isabella Owen (8)	92
Jibril Afif (10)	93
Harvey Abbas (10)	94
Sweem Albotrus (9)	95
Sophia Mavis Andrews (11)	96
Dom Szita (10)	97
Oliver Barnes (10)	98
Laily Steele (10)	99
Marley Rampersadsing (10)	100
Dylan Haines (10)	101
Danny Jacob (10)	102
Cheryl Leung (9)	103
Georgina Sifflet (10)	104
Cian Connolly (9)	105
Manu Mackay (10)	106
Enid Drew (10)	107
Dexter Hoban (11)	108
Connie Overington (10)	109
Felix Jones (8)	110

Ella Moore (11)	111
Finley Pulham (9)	112
Daisy Rose Cockle (9) & Kit	113
Oscar Smith (9)	114
Nolah Bell (9)	115
Evie Roberts (8)	116
Nathan Fittock (9)	117
Sarah Adams (10)	118
Sofia Rezk Gobrail (10)	119

Hove Junior School, Hove

Isabel Hankinson (8)	120
Albert East (9)	123
Ellie-Ann Vu (10)	124
Scarlett Elise Shuff (8)	126
Emily Carolyne Teresa Catt (9)	128
Barney McQuillan (8)	129
Tazrian Manha (8)	130
Cleo Cory-Wright (8)	131
Esme Montano-Gray (8)	132
Victoria Gomez (8)	134
Niamh Fairclough (9)	135
Mae Vernon (9)	136
Lucy Grim (8) & Esme Dawson (8)	137
Florence Ross (8)	138
Sam Sutton (9)	139
Robbie Spink (9)	140
Indi Rose Gregory-Dickson (8)	141
Abbey Sophie Blunsum (9)	142
Imogen Allen-Goble (9)	143
Biba Mariann Greenhouse (8)	144
Armaan Reza Meah (8)	145
Bronte Snell (8)	146
Akisha Miah (8)	147
Matilda Weatherall (8)	148
Poppy Maynard Rooks (8)	149
Elijah Frier (8)	150
Luca Forsyth (8)	151
Etta Moxon (8)	152
Kaci Maria Cooper (9)	153
Larnii Corrass (9)	154
Jess Baker (8)	155

Arian Vakili (8)	156
William James Chamberlain (8)	157
Lola Lemée (8)	158
Leo Maxwell Locke (9)	159
Christian Carsane (9)	160
Juliette Monica Long (9)	161
Ada Kara (9)	162
Harry Frederick Boyce (8)	163

Our Lady Of Sion Junior School, Worthing

Abigail May Wallace (7)	164
Rose Lambie (7)	165
Isaac David Coren (8)	166
Mia Louise Gokool (7)	167
Miya Croft (7)	168
Lola May Mortiboys (7)	169
Jack Isaac Seggery (7)	170
Amelie Victoria Chapman (7)	171

Shinewater Primary School, Langney

Skye Pooley (10)	172
Abdurahman Halimah (10)	174
Dominic Lewis Laureles (10)	175
Lewis Nicol (10)	176
Dinh Phu Binh Andrew Tran (10)	177
Lillia-Mae McClarence-Hart (10)	178
Lacey Julie Palmer (11)	179
Elektra Sabattini (10)	180
Marissa Ansah (11)	181
Luca Buckland (11)	182
Amy Batchelor (10)	183
Louise Perkins (10)	184

St Thomas A Becket Catholic Primary School, Eastbourne

Jasmin Barrow (9)	185
Dominik Stasik (9)	186
Chloe Rubit (10)	188
Zara Fear (9)	190

Izzy Smith (9)	192
Ahana Lukose (10)	194
Melissa Sara Mathew (10)	196
Eve Machache (9)	197
Anabel Murphy (11)	198
Gareth Gagante (10)	200
Jayden Camilleri (9)	201
Hayley Francisca Adjei Flores (9)	202
Erin McCabe (10)	203
Morgan Hooper (9)	204
Rory Fitzgerald (9)	205
Alfie Thomas (9)	206
Shelby Scaria Thomas (10)	207
Pablo Haylock-Fernandez (10)	208
Julia Antonina Karas (11)	209
Leon Holland (10)	210
Liam Alexander Collins-Sperring (9)	211
Annamaria Manoj (9)	212
Syntyche Juvan Obra (9)	213
Jess Wren (9)	214
Daniel Evans (9)	215

Telscombe Cliffs Primary School, Telscombe Cliffs

| Liberty Kemp (10) | 216 |

The Gatwick School, Crawley

Teddie Rand (8)	217
Edward Ramyar-Gulienetti (7)	218
Amaiyah Edwards (7)	220
Emily Butcher (7)	221
Kayden Forder (7)	222
Aisha Khan (7)	223

THE POEMS

The Zombie

There once was a zombie, he ate fish food,
He lived in a giant fish container.
His owner lived in a cottage in West Ham
And took him for walks on a lead.
Everyone wanted to pet him,
But when they did, they lost their fingers!
Then the owner would say,
"What did you do this time?"

Jaxon Nuttall (9)
Cornfield School, Littlehampton

Water

Levi swimming in the water,
Salt splashing in my face,
Iggy eating crickets the size of a fence
at the water,
Ned and some lobsters
Sitting near the rocks,
Snapping their claws.

Tyler Ridgley (9)
Cornfield School, Littlehampton

The Wolf

A solitary figure with ashen fur,
across the plains she runs, a blur.
With golden slits, her glinting eyes
glance up to the cloudy skies.
Cracked and thickly padded paws,
yellowed teeth and clamped jaws.
Blades of ribs press through thick fur,
her bones, wearier than they ever were.
Now she follows the sinking sun,
knowing her haunting's never done
and stealthily she slinks away,
hungry for delicious prey.
An unfed creature, malnourished and thin,
only just surviving, waiting to begin.
A flicker in her eyes, a rustle in a bush,
she prepares for her great ambush.
She leaps, paws swiping, trying to snatch,
but misses; leaves without a catch.
As the scene changes from dusk to dawn,
the wolf keeps prowling on all morn.

Phoebe Elizabeth Richards (11)
Cottesmore School, Buchan Hill

First Horse On Mars

Elephants are grey, but they don't eat hay
Although they may if they wish on a dish
But that's really for a horse of course
And that's when our story begins,
When Bob the horse was playing with a hinge.
The bee was playing with a key,
The key jolted and Bob bolted out of sight
The rocket's pocket opened
And Bob galloped inside.
An hour later, Bob was staring at the moon
While eating with a spoon.
Where was Bob? He was on Mars
Eating Galaxy bars, let's stop this.
He walked on Mars and gazed at the stars.

Daisy Andrews (9) & Mathilde Anthony
Cottesmore School, Buchan Hill

Magic Underwater

Under the water, below the tide,
Lives creatures of all sorts, all kinds.
Big and small, no matter what size,
They all have big hearts inside.
So stop putting plastic in the sea
Because it hurts outside and in the heart,
It hurts us as well because
Each creature you kill,
You kill a piece of the world
Which is a piece of life.
The colours they bring
Are colourful and sweet,
We don't want it to be sour and weak,
So stop throwing the plastic in the sea.
Thank you.

Nancy Revill (10) & Julia Kirk
Cottesmore School, Buchan Hill

Meeting Zeus

I have waited so long
To meet the king of gods.
He was big and strong
And didn't hang around for long
And he sang me a song
And it went on
And, while I was listening,
There was a big pong.
Who did it? Not me.
I thought it was that giant flea
Sat upon my knee
And I fled away with the giant flea.

Lily Aird (9)
Cottesmore School, Buchan Hill

Mustard Custard

Steaming custard that tastes like mustard
So obscene, it'll turn you green.
Once you taste it, you'll have to waste it,
Because it's so disgusting,
It belongs in a dustbin.
It bubbles away like a tasty treat
And makes you believe it's good to eat.
But don't be fooled by its creamy yellow
For I can tell you it's not that mellow.
It can't be made better
With a chocolate pudding underneath
For it's far more suited to a slice of beef
And I wouldn't try to sweeten it
With a squeeze of lemon
But you might get away with a piece of gammon.
So, when my mum puts custard on my plate,
I know it is time to make my escape.

Chloe Louise Miller (8)
Guestling Bradshaw CE Primary School, Guestling

The Fairy

Evie sat, reading in her secret den,
All was quiet and peaceful, but then
She thought she heard a little voice
Saying, "Cupcakes or cookies? It's your choice!"
She looked around her, but nothing was in sight,
So she went back to her book,
Thinking it was alright.
But, she heard the voice again,
Calling, "Come on! It's nearly time for tea!"
So she looked down to see
A sweet fairy with her hands on her hips
And beautiful wings with silvery tips.
Evie said in a quiet voice,
"Are you really real?"
"Of course I'm real, now come on!
The oven's probably burning my scone!"
The fairy led Evie to the old willow tree
And said politely,
"Would you like to have tea with me?"
"I'd love to!" said Evie delightedly.
"Come in then," answered the fairy,

And then told Evie that her name was Mary.
They went in through a little door
And Evie gasped when she saw
A table laid with delicious treats,
Cookies, doughnuts, cupcakes and sweets,
Gingerbread men and mouth-watering jellies,
All kinds of goodies to fill hungry bellies.
"I'm sorry, the chairs are so small,
It probably won't be very comfortable
For you are so tall!"
After dinner, Evie said with a sigh,
"I'm afraid its time to say goodbye,
Thank you for that lovely tea
And your kindness in sharing it with me.
But I must go home to my mother
And my dad and my dog and my brother.
They must be worried sick by now."
Mary said goodbye with a smile and a bow.
So Evie went home to another tea
And her mother was surprised to see
Her daughter clutch her stomach and flee,
Crying, "Oh Mother, I'm not hungry!"

Charis Rebecca Lane (8)
Guestling Bradshaw CE Primary School, Guestling

Chatterbox Bin

Strong, sturdy, green you see,
Best to wheel me than to smell me,
Look, be grateful, I give you no grief,
For I am cool and barely seen!

But hold on, wait a mo. Listen carefully
For I have secrets inside my lid,
Lift it carefully, there is a noise.
"Not in here!" shout screaming plastics,
"Don't you read!" moan the peelings,
Have some feelings for us in here.
We are not wanted, have no use and
are abandoned,
Chewed, squished, scrunched up and cracked.
Look more carefully to see our gold,
Be bold, there's more to us than just mould.

Chatter we do, wishing to be new,
We don't want to be stirred into a big stew,
Think about what we could be, if only you dared,
Think about our use, we don't like mixing with
manky, old juice.

Recycling is the buzz today,
Help us go the right way,
Using the colour bins
Will stop us from making a right old din.

Togetherness is not our thing,
Curry and cardboard is not a good mix.
Dustbin collectors come out at six,
Reversing their van over the bricks.
No one wants mountainous junk
Because it makes a world of gunk.
Fight back, join our team,
Become a chatterbox to help us win!

Jake James-Bell (10)
Guestling Bradshaw CE Primary School, Guestling

Wild Animals

I love to bask in the warmth of the sun,
But whenever I do, someone spoils my fun!
You think I'm special because I'm tall,
But that's not what's best about me at all!
My best feature is my tongue,
It is the longest out of everyone!
Don't laugh at me, it isn't right,
Just because I can't take flight.
I am a bird, I really am,
Why does life have to be tough?
The food I get is never enough!
It runs away and makes me chase it,
I wish it would stay still so I could taste it!
Look at those silly and funny monkeys
on the ground,
They are the strangest ones around.
All I do is eat a lot, but how I wish for a tasty treat,
Bamboo for breakfast, bamboo for lunch,
Bamboo for us all, I munch and crunch.
And bamboo for dinner, I wish I could try
something new,

I love my human, they are so kind,
But why doesn't she leave me behind?
But, when the Christmas tree is here,
She doesn't leave, she stays right here.
I wish that Christmas tree could stay,
Then she could stay every day!

Lynda-Mai Delonnette (8)
Guestling Bradshaw CE Primary School, Guestling

My Pet Cookie

My pet cookie is the size of a wookie,
By day, he's just an average treat,
By night, it is so big, it can crush a seat!
It all began two years ago,
Underneath my house, deep down below,
I was trying to make some cookies for a bake sale,
But it all went wrong.
I found a cookie crumb trail
Leading to the kitchen,
He was sorting through the fridge,
Making a giant bridge
Out of food and sweets and fruit everywhere,
He had eaten them in a flash
With half of it in his hair!
I was scared, I was worried,
I was alone and afraid,
What if something went wrong
When he was made?
So I held out my hand right there on the spot
And he gave me some food, he'd had a lot!
Since then, we've been best friends,

Just me and him together,
We made a den, just for us,
Although this all seemed like a dream,
Together, we make the perfect team!

Bonnie Cuff (10)
Guestling Bradshaw CE Primary School, Guestling

Unicorns

Going through a rainbow
Wishing I could eat it,
Then I saw an animal.
It had a horn
And I soon realised *it's a unicorn!*
It said, "Want to go through a rainbow?"
I said, "That would be kind of you."
Soon we were riding through a rainbow.
I said some words, she changed the universe,
Glitter fell from the sky.
I started to cry.
She tapped me, then I started to turn into a
unicorn,
I loved our horns.
My name was Melanie, her name was Daisy,
Sometimes, she was lazy.
She gave me a big smile,
I could see her rainbow teeth.
Unicorns are real in our hearts,
Believe in them.

Melanie Allen (8)
Guestling Bradshaw CE Primary School, Guestling

Whose View?

"It's dark up here," said the rocket to the house.
"It's darker than you at night."
"It's light down here," said the house to the rocket.
"It's as light as when you've landed."
"You are lucky," said the house.
"You can see the world up there!
But, I suppose, out of my window,
I can see so many bright colours."
The rocket exclaimed, "I can only see the stars
And the sun out of my window."
They decided to swap,
To see out of each other's windows
But, after all, they knew their own view was best.

Jessamy Read (8)
Guestling Bradshaw CE Primary School, Guestling

Space Of Talent

When I was in space, I saw a big race,
It started to rain. As I looked up,
It was the tears of Saturn.
The planet was full of emotional faces.
As the races began,
The stars started to shoot like flaming fire
In the background, Jupiter, with its excited face
Gave the beauty of the heat.
I roller-booted in my black, glowing space boots
Going so fast that rainbows pushed out the back.
As I finished the race, I slid down the banana slide
On my pancake mat,
Falling into the tears of Saturn.

Isla Goodman (8)

Guestling Bradshaw CE Primary School, Guestling

As Morning Comes

Morning comes too quickly
And I'm hanging, thinking
Between dreamy sleep
And new day's frantic rush.
I'm silently battling with images I thought I saw
Again, I feel the darkness
And the loneliness.
I hear the low, haunting sound
Breathing.
A distant gurgling.
Getting closer, louder, clearer.
I see it.
I see it!

But it's only my pet,
No need to fret.
Maximus,
As big as a house,
As gentle as a mouse.

Oh imagination!

Poppy-May Murfin (10)
Guestling Bradshaw CE Primary School, Guestling

Tea In The Bog!

Croak the frog lived in a dirty, old bog,
Brutus the dog was a really brutal dog.
Brutus said to Croak the frog,
"I don't like the smell of your dirty, old bog."
Croak the frog said, "Go away you dirty, old dog."
But Brutus the dog fell in the bog.
Croak the frog said,
"Now you smell like a dirty, old bog."
So Brutus the dog whacked Croak the frog
Into the smelly bog,
They both laughed and had tea in the bog.

Ruby Langford (9)
Guestling Bradshaw CE Primary School, Guestling

Swimming In A Pool With Unicorns

Who said unicorns aren't real?
'Cause people know we have a big deal,
I've got to say, it's getting filled with hair,
But seriously, I don't care
As long as they... Oh, I'm too late.
Wait... This is great!
The unicorn poo is making the pool blue,
It's better than a sparkling loo!
Oh thank you unicorn poo,
Oh no, they've gone crazy!
Now I have a hoof on my bum,
This wasn't much fun.

Crystal Louise Hammond (8)
Guestling Bradshaw CE Primary School, Guestling

The Amazing Unicorns!

U nicorns are as fluffy as the fluffiest cloud!
N earby always but you never hear a sound.
I ncredible creature which makes magic glow,
C osmic light which flows.
O utstanding beauty which clearly shines,
R osie loves unicorns all the time!
N ature is cool, but unicorns are better,
S o meet a unicorn so you can write her a letter! I will love unicorns forever and ever!

Rosie Barlow (8)
Guestling Bradshaw CE Primary School, Guestling

Spinosaurus Wizard

The spinosaurus is my very best friend
He is a wizard with spells, he can mend.
He lives on the moon under a lake
And he has a pet megalodon snake.
I go to see him on cold nights for tea
And he uses his magic
To make fantastic things for me.

Sonny-Mac Symes (7)
Guestling Bradshaw CE Primary School, Guestling

Flying On An Eagle

Have you ever seen an eagle fly?
It spreads its wings like a kite.
I had a dream that I was on its back,
Flying to the sun and back.
Through the clouds we'd go
And where we'd stop, only the eagle would know.

Tyler Elliott (7)
Guestling Bradshaw CE Primary School, Guestling

Candy Land

One summer's day, when I was dreaming away,
I discovered a mysterious pathway.
I saw over the hedge and a little gummy bear said,
"What a glorious day! Oh hey, are you lost?"
I replied with a yes and thought I was going west,
But I must have gotten carried away.
Oh how I loved this magical place!
It's even cooler than space!
Oh, the colourful clouds,
How they give me the wows.
The smooth, flying show, I didn't want to go!
The grass smelled of sour lemon
That made me feel like I was dancing in heaven.
In the distance, I could see a big volcano waiting
for me,
It was a long trip and I nearly broke my hip
But I made it in time to find bubbling hot chocolate
That smelled divine,
Suddenly, I woke up in a shock
And felt like I'd been hit by a rock.

Aimee Bishop (9)
Hove Junior School, Hove

The Thing In The Shed

Inspired by Skellig

The creature, the thing in the shed,
The guy,
He haunts me when I'm in bed,
I cry.

I think that he's coming up the stair,
I lie there awaiting him,
I worry so much but I say I don't care,
I feed him through the bin.

I feel that if I don't give him food,
He'll gobble me up head first,
And I really hope this won't ruin your mood,
But I think my house is cursed.

I see the shed door open wide,
Slowly, I tiptoe in.
"If you're there, come out, don't hide."
"Do you have an aspirin?"

Shocked I was that he replied,
Though aspirin, I had none.

Away from the shed I began to stride,
"If you want an aspirin, get one!"

Then, on my leg, I felt a hand,
Cold and wet with sweat.
And little did I understand,
That now he posed a threat.

"Chinese takeaway is what I need,
So fetch it for me now!
An aspirin and a book to read,
Just bring it here somehow!"

So out I hurried from the shed
To fetch what he desired.
"Food of the gods," he said.
But he did not know it expired!

Sofia Challis Sanches (10)
Hove Junior School, Hove

The Creature In The Garage - Skellig

Inspired by Skellig

An eerie silence falls beyond,
Rotten stenches hit me,
A weakening light so fond of darkness,
Murdering all sign of glee.
Bumbling bricks seize their hold so tight
To prevent themselves from falling,
An abandoned shed so far from bright,
All misery is calling.

A blanket of grey to shield the mould,
When kitchen units hold the worst,
No living soul to be told,
Pass through doors and they shall be cursed.
Silver spiders' webs to grasp one's clothes,
The hum of diving flies,
Small rodents scuttle, whom cleaners loathe
A pale, crinkled body lies.

An overwhelming chill runs down my spine,
Long, jewelled, bloody lips hold still,
Wilting walls so sharp like vines,
Coils of cold create a chill.
The helpless soul lies all alone,
Too weak to put up a fight,
A neglected statue as tough as bone
So still through day and night.

Gabrielle Moteane-Lyefook (11)

Hove Junior School, Hove

Standing There

Inspired by Skellig

Lying there in the corner,
All alone, by himself,
How sad it is, he is a mourner,
Crouching there under the shelf.

Blue bottles and flies in his hair,
Veins all over his face,
Sitting there, he doesn't care,
Good memories he will erase,
He lives in people's nightmares.

He eats spiders, lice and fleas,
Grim thoughts fill his head,
Standing there, you must agree,
He'll watch you on your deathbed.

Sitting there, oh so slim,
He'll whisper in your ear.
Imagine him, his face so grim,
Filling you with fear.

Crouching there in despair,
He stands small and shy,
His voice in your head will blare,
Talk to him with no reply.

Lying there, motionless
Can you hear a heartbeat?
I don't think so.

Mabel Heather Chapman-Smith (10)

Hove Junior School, Hove

Lollipop

I see a lollipop,
It's blue and pink,
It's in the sea,
Now, will it sink?

No, it won't!
It's coming to me!
It's riding the waves
Like a surfer at sea!

Oh no, I'm here
In the lollipop!
What shall I do?
I can't climb up!

Oh look, turn around,
It's 3008,
I'm in the future,
Oh, what a surprise!

Chocolate is here,
Sweets are there

And there are icing drops
In that tree.

Now I know
Where I am
Yes, you're right,
I'm in a fantasy land!

Turn around, see that moon
And a dragon drinking its milk,
Look on its horn,
Floating in midair.

Oh my, oh what,
How could this be?
That dragon is now
My property!

Amira Djemaoun (9)
Hove Junior School, Hove

Mermaid Cat Vs Mermaid Dog

Killer cat in the ocean,
Causing a great commotion.
Miaow, miaow,
Hiss, hiss,
No time to make a big twist,
Cats and dogs don't go well together.
They are not best friends forever,
No one knew it was a misadventure
A big, old cat licking her lips,
A mean, old dog shaking his hips.
Purr, purr,
Miaow, miaow,
Mermaid Dog's about to say, "Ow!"
Ocean cops have some cat chow,
Sea police, act now!
They're in prison yet again,
Luckily, I had a pen,
Mermaid Cat's about to see freedom!

Luckily, she didn't need them,
Right now, she's stuck to the door,
About to pounce right to the core
Of a hopeless ocean filled with dogs
Hopefully there's no fog!

Maya Rossoni (9)
Hove Junior School, Hove

Burger Meeting

B ig Mac invited me to a burger museum, I said yes.

U nder the sea, I took a chicken shrimp supreme

R ose up to the meeting and finally, I got there

G ot to say hello, his name was Beef Boss and his son was Bacon Jr.

E verything went right, we were going to take over KFC but I

R an off at a slow pace and they ran really fast!

M um was a fan of KFC, she wasn't happy at all

E verything had to restart again

E verything went good again, so we were going to take over Loose Women.

T V was fun to watch and I wished to be on there,

I was happy like a spoiled pig because I was on TV.

N ext day, it got cancelled

G od took over the show.

Isaac Lewis (9)
Hove Junior School, Hove

The Edible World!

As the stars shine bright,
I close my eyes tight...
I am eating an edible house,
Chewing on a sugar cane mouse,
Drinking a ketchup bath,
Munching a Dolly Mix path.
Sucking my candyfloss pillow,
Sitting under a pick 'n' mix willow
Eating a broccoli tree,
Licking candy cane walking sticks, three!
Biting the cookie ground,
Also the blueberry hat I found,
Chewing a chocolate pen,
Munching a vanilla hen.
Eating my delicious mug,
Mmm, that scrumptious jello bug.
I open my eyes and it's just a dream,
Oh, how I wish it was real!
But I guess I could have McDonald's
And that would do until my wish comes true!

Lily Gordon (9)
Hove Junior School, Hove

The Creature In The Garage

Inspired by Skellig

Skin as soft and wrinkly as a sponge,
Weak, powerless, dusty, really unsteady body
In a dusty garage full of gunge,
All alone in a garage, with nobody.
He has old, dusty, wrinkly arms,
His whole body is bloodless
And he has really sweaty palms
And the garage floor is mudless.
The more he moves his muscles,
The more he gets weakened.
His hands are really grubby
And, because of Arthur, he thought it was the end.
Even Michael calls him bubbly,
Sometimes the creature gets sick
And he is really thin
And, when he's eaten, he gives his plate a lick
And he smells like he lives in a bin.

Alfie Charles Ernest Joseph (10)

Hove Junior School, Hove

Entering Into The Gloom

Entering into the gloom,
His hands reached out for food,
The shadows, they just loom,
His anger spreads the mood.

His eyes are a blurry black
His black suit is as dark as night
All the animals curled up in the grimy shack,
His face is as pale as white.

Dust is all over his face,
He haunts my dreams every night.
He crawls upstairs at a tremendous pace,
The place is such a fright.

His creaky voice clogged with dust replays like a
record player,
The crunch of his bones are ever so slight,
The dust formed into a thick layer,
The crunch echoed with a burdensome bite.

Ginger Kurzel (11)
Hove Junior School, Hove

Monster Loud Events

Hear the pit crews tinker! Grangle!
Hear old cars moan and groan! Mangle!

See the smoke whirl! Float!
See the zombies boast! Gloat!

Smell burning rubber!
Zombie road race!

Hear the propellers flow! Squeak!
Hear the petrol tanks open! Leak!

See the planes whoosh! Zoom!
See the big tankers clatter! Loom!

Smell rocket flame!
Skeleton airshow!

Hear the boats sucker! Spluck!
Hear the sea cook up a whirlpool! Suck!

See the boats go! Splash!
See the sea fall on the rocks! Crash!

Smell the sea air!
Squid motorboat race!

Jude WatersRugman (9)

Hove Junior School, Hove

Skellig

Inspired by Skellig

A creature sitting in my garage,
He sat there like a big mirage,
He had a cracked, pale face and weak bones,
Noises echoing like moans and groans.

Twenty-seven and fifty-three,
"Nothing," he said weirdly.
This old man shouted noisily,
"Twenty-seven and fifty-three!"

Twenty-seven dripping from his lip,
Fifty-three on the cold floor,
Doesn't leave because he doesn't have friends,
No one comes to the door.

Hiding black wings behind his back,
Just in case of an attack,
A thin, black suit wrapped around him,
It seemed very slim.

Maia Cristina Kaur Colombini (10)
Hove Junior School, Hove

Looming In The Darkness

Inspired by Skellig

His deep, black eyes as dark as evil,
His face shuddering with the moonlight.
The bare sun rose too fast for retrieval,
His eyes like most had been set alight.

His scarce, walking demons,
His face shattered within the dusk air,
Haunting a shadowy landscape gleam,
A black suit he claims he must wear.

Full of the dimmest dares,
A silhouette, completely markless,
Such a creature must be so rare,
Looming in the darkness.

From what I have discovered,
His eyes glinted a dull shade of grey,
But what lay undiscovered
Was only a day away.

Lily Rose Britton (10)
Hove Junior School, Hove

The Creature In The Garage

Inspired by Skellig

Early morning fallen dawn,
What once was pride, now dead and gone,
With no one left to care or mourn,
Where no shard of light has ever shone.

He lies there, lined like an ancient map,
Faded eyes unblinking blue,
His life a secret kept under wraps,
An existence he failed to follow through.

Not yet dead, but barely alive,
Fading faster every day,
Only body, not soul, survives,
Slipping, slipping away.

Nobody knows he lies there,
Who he is or what he once was,
Not a soul on the Earth does care
If he dies like the rest of us.

Annie May MacPhail Matthews (10)
Hove Junior School, Hove

Celebrating Differences

Me and Bigfoot were packing our things so we
could go to Candyland.
"Argh! Wow, that was a long ride in the portal!"
We were in Candyland.
Bigfoot lifted me up so I could get the chocolate
fudges from the trees.
I said, "Ooh! I see chocolate fondue! OMG, I need a
taste of it! Come on!"
It was tasty. I also saw spicy candy.
Bigfoot shook.
"What Bigfoot? You don't like them? Why? They're
the best thing ever!"
The floor was ice cream and I could smell
pancakes.
"Okay Bigfoot, let's go to the candy hotel!"

Summer Blossom Carwin-Knox (8)
Hove Junior School, Hove

Danger In The Dark

Inspired by Skellig

A nose like a crooked harpoon
Hiding in a cockroach nest
A face as pale as the moon
It's not expecting any guests

Knotted knuckles and a crumbling spine
A half-dead skeleton lies in the corner
Thin toes tangled like grapevine
With a black slit that was for a mourner.

Slim, slender and dirty,
Eating flies and black spiders
A thing with no mercy
Bad luck will come to the finders.

The scraggly hairs on its skin
With a rotten name like Arthur
It might like some simple gin
But it wants a happy ever after.

Dov Zanardo (10)
Hove Junior School, Hove

Skellig

Inspired by Skellig

Skellig, the man with a creased, cracked face
Skellig, the man with matchstick bones
Skellig, the creature who doesn't know his place
Skellig, the creature who moans and groans
Skellig, the beast who doesn't see day
Skellig, the beast with dried, stinking sweat
Skellig, the being who never seems to play
Skellig, the being who never goes back on a threat
Skellig, the animal with a baggy, ancient suit
Skellig, the animal with grimy, colourless hair
Skellig, the angel with broken, old boots
Skellig, the angel who doesn't ever care.

Amara Jogee (11)
Hove Junior School, Hove

Genie Cat

My genie cat is very nice,
It gives me a lot of advice,
We live in a lamp which is really big,
Her favourite food is a big fig.
We have a nice sofa, even a bath
And also, we have a golden path.
The curtains are pink pearls
Which have a bit of a curl.
I have a big bed with the world's biggest ted.
My cat has a basket which is so soft
Like the pillows from the loft.
We have a kitchen with a lot of food,
I have a mug that says something rude,
People have to rub my home to get me out,
But I never scream and never shout.

Kate Moore (9)
Hove Junior School, Hove

The Vacuum

Inside the vacuum
Will give you a tantrum
You will see unbelievably
All the stuff will fill you with dread
Your brain will whirl around in your head
The dirt will annoy your throat
You will act like a goat
You'll kick and scream and let out some steam
The objects of lost, you will find
And you will feel all kind
But that's not all
You will escape the impossible cape
And you will jump out
And shout, "Hooray!
I'm out at last!"
But not for long
As I get sucked up for another song.

Ethan Smith (9)
Hove Junior School, Hove

The Creature In The Garage!

Inspired by Skellig

Behind the garage near the tea chest,
There's an old man having a rest.

He has cracked, old skin and bones that are thin
And doesn't like anyone who bothers him.

He lived next to a van
And beside him there was a wheel
I thought he was dead, but no, he was real.

Behind his jacket, there were thin bones,
Maybe he's an angel, nobody knows.

Twenty-seven and fifty-three,
That's all he wanted out of me,
So I grabbed the money, I grabbed the cash
And, in a flash, I had it!

Veronica Calvert (10)

Hove Junior School, Hove

The Witches' Picnic

Up in the clouds,
Way above your heads,
The witches are getting ready.
They are getting ready for a picnic,
A picnic so gruesome,
You would probably die.
For in their cauldron they are mixing,
Frog's skin to give it some spice.
Lizard's tongue for flavour.
A warthog's heart as a main ingredient,
And a little drop of fly's blood.

Now, I think you can see why,
I told you not to go,
I don't know about you, but if I went,
You probably wouldn't see me for a week!

Lily Chauhan (9)
Hove Junior School, Hove

The Crazy Animal And Nugget Rap Boi!

As the sun rises,
The cow pat is here,
While Farmer Charlie is drinking beer!
Over in the forest,
The sky is blue,
You can't see the demon chameleon
Doing a poo.
While Farmer Charlie
Is having a nap,
The old chicken nugget
Starts to rap!
"Hey! What's up dog?
More like hot dog!
Heey!
I'm feeling crispy, bro!"
Little cow Jub was born in a jug,
When she grew old,
She went quite mad,

A few days later, she became
A psychopath!

Sidney Bell (10) & Lyla Hunt (10)
Hove Junior School, Hove

Lollipop Story

Poppy read a story
Full of lollipop glory,
Each lollipop was different,
It was much better than any other book.
Then Poppy began to look
At the teacher, writing a maths equation,
Not much of a sensation.
She stared at the lollipop bear,
She licked the bear
And fell into the dare,
Then saw a lollipop pear!
"I'm in the swirl! I fell out of the world!
What do I do? I'm doomed! I'm doomed!"
She was in a maze,
Not in a haze.
"What do I do?"

Delilah Edinburgh (9)
Hove Junior School, Hove

The Earth Is A Giant Cookie

If you look at the Earth,
Try not to surf
Because soon, you will fail to see
The Earth in all of its glory.
For it will be a chocolate chip cookie.
All of the splodges in its chocolatey goodness
Are all edible for you to eat
For more of its foodiness
Are all worth its chewiness.
After all, you see a chocolate stream
As nice as it may be, there is no gravity
As a cookie decides what it does
If this planet is food, you may have a clue
That every other planet is too!

Freya Noakes (9)
Hove Junior School, Hove

Come To The Bat Light Show!

L et's go have some fun
I n the cave with the bats everyone!
G rab your glow sticks and glowing stuff!
H ow do the bats do so many memorable things,
T o impress us all at the light show?

S winging around upside down, can you hear the cheering crowd?
H ow do they do it all?
O h, it's so peculiar that they don't seem to hate light, can you see the beautiful light?
W ell, how did you enjoy the fluttery bat light show?

Alex Colocolov (9)

Hove Junior School, Hove

There's A Monster In The Mushroom

A monster lives in the mushroom,
His life must be full of gloom.

He has a pumpkin as a pet,
Imagine taking him to the vet!

His carriage is the strangest of all,
It looks like a massive ball.

Have you ever lived in a mushroom?
Have you had a life full of gloom?

Have you ever had a pumpkin as a pet?
Have you taken *him* to the vet?

Have you been a monster,
That looks like a lobster,
Riding a motorised moon?

Sophie Martine Warner (9)
Hove Junior School, Hove

The Creature

Inspired by Skellig

His bloodshot eyes staring deep into mine
His straggly hair framing his face
His rattling breath sending chills up my spine
Sitting in a dark, gloomy place.

His black suit covering his slim frame
His leather boots all worn
The same things he's been wearing since he came
His words are as short and as sharp as a thorn.

I cannot properly hear him
As he whispers some sort of curse
His laugh so dark and grim
His face pinched and terse.

Iris O'Brien (10)
Hove Junior School, Hove

Nature Is Alive!

Step on the crunchy leaves
Gaze at the twisting trees
Hear the squirrels squeak
Watch the oldest tree creak
The butterflies flitter and flutter
The mud is slippery like butter
Vines hanging from the blue
The forest knows what to do...

Suddenly, there was a *bang!*
A crash, a slam
The bushes started to dance
The leaves jumped and pranced
The trees began to bash
The mud does a *smash!*

The forest is alive.

Mia Kruppa (9)
Hove Junior School, Hove

The Awakening Of The Speedstar

One night, there was a scary sight,
Lightning struck strongly,
Wobbly people got stuck in a coma,
Some people were so scared, they ran to Roma.
Weirdly, people woke up eight months later
with powers
They got fed and they realised they were strong.
One man woke up with super speed,
He felt the need to run and help people,
But most people were just like him
They wanted to kill and get a load of cash,
But the Speedstar showed no fear and helped!

Freddy Hartin-McQuade (9)
Hove Junior School, Hove

Pigzilla Is In Town

The crowd's cheering is very loud,
A big monster enters the field,
It gives the commentators
A big appearance.

Old Joe says, "Yo!"
Pigzilla goes, "Oink!"
"Hey! That's not a nice way
To speak!"

Fizztingler, bottle-squasher,
The chocolate dragon comes to help
They fight all night
Until the clock strikes midnight.
The chocolate dragon falls.

Pigzilla stares into the night.

Harry Goodwin (9) & Alfie Jury (9)
Hove Junior School, Hove

Eyes Of Jade

In the ebony void of dust,
Blinking eyes of jade
Like a flare of auric fire
In the heavens made.

The vast, inky blackness
That lay beneath those eyes
Was unfathomable, unknown
Like a night without the skies.

Swept into the void
Of the blinking, jade eyes
Through the cloak of dust
Those glinting, blinking eyes.

My house, my city,
My world is all gone.
But those blinking eyes
Are blinking as one.

Alonna Flexer-Sandiland (11)
Hove Junior School, Hove

I'm On My Own In The Freezing Cold

I made a new friend on my trip
He was nice and fluffy
He loves to know he's cuddly
But suddenly,
I was with him underwater
I think almost a quarter
But I floated up to land
Woah! He held his breath for long!
He was probably gone
I was on my own in the freezing cold
I bet he was catching seals
Or maybe he met a female
I was on my own in the freezing cold
He was all fluffy and cuddly
And I was all cold and shivery.

Georgia Lawmon (8)
Hove Junior School, Hove

The Creature

Inspired by Skellig

A face filled with creases
What a scary sight,
Arms like dog leashes
I'd give you a fright.

I've got skin that is as white as paper,
I am the scariest creature of them all.
You'll never want to see me later,
I'd stick out even at a poor people's ball.

In my eyes, I've got red scary veins,
I wear old and stinky clothes,
If you see me, I'll bring back the pain,
I swear on all of my oaths.

Freya Molloy (10)
Hove Junior School, Hove

The Garage

Inspired by Skellig

Under the house, near the garage
And in the garage, there was a man.
Behind the chests, behind the old carriage,
He lived next to an old man.
Right next to him was an old wheel,
I thought he was dead, but no, he was real
Twenty-seven and fifty-three
That's all he wanted from me.
Behind his jacket were thin bones,
Maybe he is an angel, nobody knows.
He smelled like blue bottles and spiders
But you can tell he is an outsider.

Emre Gokmen (10)

Hove Junior School, Hove

The Creature In The Garage

His slender body, thin as sticks,
With a nose like a harpoon,
Looking like he's about to kick,
A face as pale as the moon.

A neck covered in snail's grime,
With a white, bloodless face,
It hides in a corner all the time,
And it sits on the top of a suitcase.

With rancid, rotten, serrated teeth,
A baffled look grew on its face,
Half of it under a sheath,
It shows as much emotion as a mace.

Luka Bowles (10)
Hove Junior School, Hove

The Creature In The Garage

Inspired by Skellig

With depleted perspiration on his forehead
Bouquet of flakes
The undetected man sat there, nearly dead.
He suddenly awakes
Bleached aspect from sitting in the
untouched garage
Rotten teeth and wizened cartilage.
The old owner did unforgettable damage
In a mysterious, unknown village
Where nobody knows.
There's a man called Arthur
Where all this junk goes
But all he really wants is a happy ever after.

Mel Cappelle Mendes (10)
Hove Junior School, Hove

Skellig

Inspired by Skellig

His eyes a web of scarlet veins
Pale, cracked skin as white as bone
His body wracked with awful pains
Sits in the garage all alone.

He keeps me awake at night
He always laughs but never smiles
His face is never in the light
He may have travelled many miles.

I don't know a thing about him
What did he do to make him pay?
Did he commit a dreadful sin?
All he ever says is, "Go away!"

Arun Webb (10)
Hove Junior School, Hove

Man In The Garage

Inspired by Skellig

A man lay in the garage, all alone
With nothing to eat,
He was just blood and bone.
He ate bugs while drinking from jugs
But the water was dirty
With hair and guts.
Groaning and moaning, tired of life,
His name was forgotten and full of lies.
Dark, black suit and mangled hair
He looked no better than a bear,
But nobody knew of his extraordinary wings
Which flew so beautifully through the wind.

Natalie Kiara Kocaiova (10)

Hove Junior School, Hove

Skellig

Inspired by Skellig

The creature that lives in the shed,
Both wings are hidden away
I dream about him in bed
I discovered him yesterday.
Tiny creases and cracks
All over his pale, white face.
He shouts at little, black bats
As they fly all over the place.
Is it a dream made up in my head?
Could he be what he seems?
Looking so ill, almost dead,
"Twenty-seven and fifty-three,
Aspirin if you please."

Abigail Lish (10)
Hove Junior School, Hove

Cactus On The Brain!

I got a cactus stuffed in my face,
All because I lost a race!
Its pointy spikes ran along my tongue,
Whilst the juices flowed into my tum.
It was like I was eating a banquet,
On a golden, sandy blanket.
Next, I saw a scary snake,
With jagged teeth like a rake,
It stared at me in awe,
While I had cactus in my jaw.
When I ran, it was against Peter Pan,
He flew away, and taunted me the next day!

Amy Carrigan (9)
Hove Junior School, Hove

Skellig

Inspired by Skellig

Red veins in his eyes
Face as pale as the moon
He was covered in flies
On this dreadful afternoon.

His dusty, black suit
His few colourless hairs
His lonesome boot
Nobody even cared.

Knuckles were swollen
Fingers were twisted
His heart had been stolen
I didn't know he existed.

He always laughed
But never smiled
Such a sight
For such a small child.

Thea Stott (10)
Hove Junior School, Hove

The Creature In The Dark...

Inspired by Skellig

Cracks and creases fill his face,
Knuckles swollen, red and raw.
In his suit is so much more,
Oh, that thing is very poor.

Face like plaster, old and white,
Smothered sauce upon his lip.
Sits in the dark, scared of light,
In the shed is like a tip.

A net of bloodshot eyes,
Sometimes he laughs, but never smiles.
In the garage, there he lies,
Behind piles of patterned tiles.

Anoushka Millie Musgrave (11)

Hove Junior School, Hove

The Shed...

The rickety, old thing just stood there,
Should I really go in?
Should I really dare?
This place is like a human being
Moss and grime coating this wooden shed.
Reluctantly, I open the decomposing door,
I could see the body of a man who was dead.
He sickened me to the core,
Long, twisted fingernails,
A strong, pungent smell,
I could hear his weird wails,
This place is like hell...

Iestyn James (10)
Hove Junior School, Hove

Skellig

Inspired by Skellig

His life was all rotten,
He didn't live it well,
His name was forgotten
While he hid in a shell.

He wants to be ordinary,
Instead, he's all rotten,
His wings are extraordinary,
He's almost forgotten.

He wishes he could eat food,
His favourites are twenty-seven and fifty-three.
At times he can be very rude,
But it's because he wants to be free!

Zach Jude Whittingham (10)

Hove Junior School, Hove

A Vile Man

Inspired by Skellig

Red lips as scarlet as blood
His eyes, a web of veins
His white suit darkened by mud
His illness gave him pains.

He smelled of extremely old dust
I thought he was dead at first
Sauce on his mouth began to crust
His lie was the worst.

He had a tangled nest of hair
He laughed but never smiled
It looked like he was in despair
So creepy for a young child.

Grace Wells (10)

Hove Junior School, Hove

Rainbow Lava

R ed, orange, yellow, green and blue
A round the terrified girl
I n a burning volcano
N obody could help her
B ut, luckily, she could breathe
O n the bottom of the volcano
W ho would save her?

L ife or death? She cried
"A rgh!"
V icious volcano sucked her up
A nd she never returned.

Ellie Wright (9)

Hove Junior School, Hove

The Trouble With Roald Dahl Books

James, Charlie and George
One peach, one factory, one medicine.

James, the poor kid
With two aunties,
One fat, one slim
And both with a horrible grin.

Charlie, his mum, his dad,
All glad when he found
A fifty pence piece on the ground.

George, that funny, little boy,
He gave his grandma a real good fright,
She barely even slept at night!

Amelie Bourne (10)
Hove Junior School, Hove

Movies

M y mouth tasted like salt

O ur emotions came, but Peppa Pig was sad

V ideos came on but Peppa Pig's nose just shot out more and more snot.

I smelled popcorn from behind my back

"E at it!" said Peppa Pig and I ate the popcorn from Peppa Pig's tiny hands

"S sh!" said the crowd as Peppa Pig shouted, "That's me!"

Maisy Standing (9)

Hove Junior School, Hove

Creature In The Garage

Inspired by Skellig

In a filthy place full of rust,
Lay a creature that was extremely little
And covered head to toe in dust
With bones extremely weak and brittle.

In this garage behind the chest
Was a ravenous beast,
Separated from the rest,
Dreaming of a feast.

A unique creature,
One of a kind
With crooked knuckles as a feature
Who eats Chinese to unwind.

Harry Luke Kinsey (10)
Hove Junior School, Hove

The Creature In The Garage

Inspired by Skellig

Eyes swollen and inflamed
Red veins popping
The creature was never reclaimed
And in the night, you would hear knocking.

Out in the darkness, the creature lurks
Eating spiders, blue bottles and lice
In the creepy, creepy murks
Where scuttling are mice.

His rancid breath
Fowl and disgusting
He was close to death
And the table was rusting.

Yara Penfold (10)
Hove Junior School, Hove

The Cupcake Of Doom

There was a monster
That ate a cupcake,
Then it turned into a cupcake monster
Which was very, very small.

There was a huge baby dragon
That ate a cupcake,
Then it turned into a baby dragon monster
Which was very large.

There was a talking olive
That ate a cupcake,
Then it turned into an olive monster
Which was very, very medium-sized.

Max Weightman-Achille (9)

Hove Junior School, Hove

Picnic On The Moon

As I set off to the moon,
I met a caterpillar in a cocoon
I unpacked my basket and drank my tea,
I took one sip, then one, two, three...
"Oh! Yippee!"
I thought with glee,
I'm on the moon, can't you see?
I know it sounds odd, I really do,
But this might even happen to you!
A picnic on the moon,
Whoever thought that was possible?

Sophie Rose Biggs (10)
Hove Junior School, Hove

The Mysterious Creature

Behind the tea chests,
Ancient and mouldy
A death-like image stirs,
Eating spiders, grotesque and wild.

Light or dark, friend or foe,
Who knows until it's discovered.

One way or another,
This sinister creature
Will jump out behind you
From a rotting tile.

This macabre creature's identity
Will be uncovered.

Harry Langley (10)
Hove Junior School, Hove

Hyperspace Jacob Face!

Bored from tectonic plates and China,
I wished school was fun not dumb.
Then, in the depth of my brain...
The Hyperspace Jacob Face was born!
Rushing from the fiery heart of a volcano,
Spinning through hyperspace to our school
It wished to take over
So a fight began to fizzle up.
Suddenly, the headmistress
Began a fight with a clash and a bang!

Jacob Doorly (9)
Hove Junior School, Hove

Burger Planet!

Deep in space,
Holding a mace,
A planet is out there,
But with no hair.
A planet of food,
People are there
And they call each other 'dude'.
It's a burger
So far, there's been no murder,
With a ketchup well,
That will never smell,
You can eat it
Bit by bit
And it grows back
But it will fight and attack.

Jake Cotton-Hewitt (10)
Hove Junior School, Hove

I Found Him In The Garage

Inspired by Skellig

I found him in the garage at first,
He had a broken, cracked face
And bones that were thin.
He didn't like anyone who was bothering him.

Twenty-seven and fifty-three
Were all he wanted out of me,
I grabbed the cash and, in a flash,
I had it.

I went to his place in the garage,
He told me to get out of his space,
So I did.

Lili Angus (10)
Hove Junior School, Hove

The Lost World

One day, a man came up to me
He had a bushy moustache
He said, "Do you want to go
On an island called Yslenoolou
To stop the island's volcano from exploding?"

One day later, I took a plane
My plane landed.
I found a friend called Blue,
He was a velociraptor,
He had a blue stripe
Going along his body.

Finley C (9)
Hove Junior School, Hove

The Dragon Who Drank The Moon!

Slurp, slish, slosh,
Came a sound from a dragon called Josh.
Josh was a dragon who had a dream,
His dream was to beam,
This dragon wanted a drink,
Nothing pink,
Just the moon,
Nothing amazing,
Just the moon blazing.
Just the moon,
Not with a spoon,
But come see this dragon,
Why not rent a wagon?

Emma Harrison (9)
Hove Junior School, Hove

Rainbow Slugs

Up in the sky,
Oh so high,
As the sun beamed down,
I was lying in the strangest place.
I was lying on a cloud!
As I looked up,
I looked up far
I saw a flock of rainbow slugs!
What?
The slugs were big,
The slugs were bold
And they were shiny like metallic gold!
Maybe next time, they'll be silver!

Violette Paul (9) & Dixie Probyn

Hove Junior School, Hove

Underwater Delight

As the water goes by, I think to myself
Oh why, oh why, I love to swim in the sea!
Yes, oh, let's do that then!
But I need something very delicious,
That could be pizza, yeah, pomodoro pizza!
Well, let's do that then!
Yum! The pizza's tasty,
Yum! The pizza's warm!
It is amazing!

Casper Davenport (9)
Hove Junior School, Hove

Having Lunch With An Alien

At lunch, I went down to a sunken ship
And the pirates there didn't mind a bit.
While I was sitting on a chunk of bark,
I saw something moving in the dark.
It came out of the shadows
And it came out of a space I thought was
quite narrow.
It was an alien in a wetsuit!
And he was playing a tune on his flute.

Isabella Owen (8)
Hove Junior School, Hove

The Creature - Skellig

Inspired by Skellig

Motionless and withered away,
There lives a creature in the garage today.

Twenty-seven and fifty-three are food from gods
And there are a lot of mods.

His lips are the colour of blood
And his face is covered in mud.

Skellig, the one who hides his wings
And has these old, weird, spinning rings.

Jibril Afif (10)
Hove Junior School, Hove

Garage Room

Looking at a room of gunge,
Thinking it needs a clean,
There's no point in doing a lunge
Unless you can work a machine.

It's a filthy room of bugs
In the corner of the room,
Be aware of all the slugs,
You will find the biggest doom.

It has bony fingers,
The smell of smoke lingers.

Harvey Abbas (10)
Hove Junior School, Hove

94

Magic Cat!

In my sleep, my cat goes *poof!*
Poof! Kaboom! Miaow and *bam!*

It jumps over the moon,
Over the stew and the loo,
I really hope it doesn't get the flu.

Once again, it goes *poof!*
Kaboom! Miaow and *bam!*
I hope it doesn't eat the ham!

Sweem Albotrus (9)
Hove Junior School, Hove

Skellig

Inspired by Skellig

He has very thin, skeletal bones
His face is cracked and pale
He doesn't go a day without a groan or a moan
And if he walked, he'd be as slow as a snail.

To everyone, he is unknown
And he's as stiff as a doornail
His teeth are covered in limestone
And he's the opposite of a whale.

Sophia Mavis Andrews (11)
Hove Junior School, Hove

Skellig

Inspired by Skellig

As I tiptoed into the ancient room,
Scuttling filled the dusty floor,
The rotten floorboards needed a good broom,
Looked like someone's a carnivore.

Twenty-seven and fifty-three spread around,
Brown ale stains everywhere,
No more scuttling, no more sound,
Then came something, a glare.

Dom Szita (10)
Hove Junior School, Hove

Skellig

Inspired by Skellig

He was dusty, old and weak,
His painful joints would only squeak.
His voice rattled when he spoke,
It was barely more than a faded croak.
I was surprised he did not die,
300 years must have gone by.

Oh, Skellig, you may be old,
But behind the grime there's a heart of gold!

Oliver Barnes (10)
Hove Junior School, Hove

The Creature In The Garage

Inspired by Skellig

In the cold, dark, rotting garage,
A creature lies,
Wanting to run away in a gleaming carriage,
Eating blue bottles and flies.

Bones like a jagged twig,
The ancient man looks so old and broken down.
His face is like a dead pig,
The chair he sits on is crumbling to the ground.

Laily Steele (10)
Hove Junior School, Hove

Skellig's Hidden Side

Inspired by Skellig

I see him in the garage,
I'm finding him a bit savage,
He wants to be ordinary,
But his wings are extraordinary.
He didn't look like he'd ever had a marriage,
Because he didn't seem very average.
I found him hairy but very scary,
And he had a friend called Mary.

Marley Rampersadsing (10)
Hove Junior School, Hove

Skellig

Inspired by Skellig

In the garage is a weird man
With cracked skin
With his wings so low.
He is weak, just like a tin man
Thinking that his wings can go,
Hating Ernie, that old man
You really call him like so
And, if he heard, he would hurt you,
Maybe even with a bow and arrow!

Dylan Haines (10)
Hove Junior School, Hove

The Giant Biscuit

When you look in the oven,
Here is what you see:

A giant biscuit with chocolate chips
Is definitely to be,
Towering ferociously all over me,
It's possibly the last thing you'll see.
It's now larger than a city,
Now chocolate has melted onto me!

Danny Jacob (10)
Hove Junior School, Hove

Celebrating Difference

Hi, I'm Betty and this is Alan,
I like ice cream and he likes chocolate,
Alan likes football but I like school,
I love learning but he hates learning,
Alan loves PE and I like art,
Alan likes swimming but I love sewing,
I love doing hair but he hates doing hair.

Cheryl Leung (9)
Hove Junior School, Hove

The Creature In The Garage

Lurking behind fossilised, chalky chests
In a garage full of webs,
Lay a creature who had been disposed,
Curled up in a ball in bed.
Green eyes stared at you like Medusa
As he sat there, looking dead
And he had a baby called Musa
Who was the happiest baby yet.

Georgina Sifflet (10)
Hove Junior School, Hove

Age Of Death

Inspired by Warhammer

As my bones melt in the blood,
As death will rise and terrorise,
As the reapers come,
And the skeletons swim,
We have no hope.
Nagash will control the seven realms,
The dead will rise from the ground,
After the Age of Death,
There will be nothing left.

Cian Connolly (9)

Hove Junior School, Hove

Skellig

Inspired by Skellig

He wants to be ordinary
Instead, he's all rotten
His wings are extraordinary
He's almost forgotten
Skellig is colourless and hairy
And I think that he must be quite bored
Others usually find him quite scary
While he sits on the broken floorboards.

Manu Mackay (10)
Hove Junior School, Hove

The Girl In The Bubble

B ubbles fly above the ocean
U nder the ocean, the party began
B ubbles began to pop!
B lue ocean simmers in the sun
L ife underwater
E legant bubbles spread over the ocean
S *plosh* went the girl.

Enid Drew (10)

Hove Junior School, Hove

In The County Hole

In the cold, he sleeps and eats
Massive settlings of lice,
Fifty-three and twenty-seven
Take away the taste of mice,
Pale skin like haunted ghosts,
The secret life he makes,
Keeping what he loves the most,
Leaving destruction in his wake.

Dexter Hoban (11)
Hove Junior School, Hove

Differences

People are different,
White or black,
Fat or thin,
People are people,
Everyone's equal,
Nothing comes in-between.
Different countries,
Many families,
We all come together as one,
On the same planet,
We shall remain.

Connie Overington (10)

Hove Junior School, Hove

George's Big Day Out

One day, I was in a spaceship and I saw an alien
I went over to the alien in my spacesuit
And I asked what its name was
And the alien said, "Jimbob."
Jimbob had green tentacles and yellow eyes,
I floated in my spaceship.

Felix Jones (8)
Hove Junior School, Hove

It's Skellig

Inspired by Skellig

He sits in the corner like an old bag,
What's he doing here, you wonder aloud.
Then he creaks, "What, you young lad?"
A blanket of dust covers his face,
You look at his clothes in such a disgrace.
It's Skellig.

Ella Moore (11)
Hove Junior School, Hove

Gaming Monsters

G aming with grumpy grandma
A nd she's worse than me
M onsters eating on the iPad
I nterestingly, I don't eat monsters
N aughty Nando ate some fruit
G reat, he's kind of like me.

Finley Pulham (9)
Hove Junior School, Hove

The Magical Cup

One summer's day, something got in my way
I picked up a cup and got a scoop of water,
I thought of a drink and there it was,
My blackcurrant squash!
It changed quickly under the cloth,
Oh how I loved my magical cup!

Daisy Rose Cockle (9) & Kit

Hove Junior School, Hove

The Tiger Made Out Of Crisps

T he busy forest in the TV
I s all melted and strange, but
G reat with a tiger made out of crisps.
E ven though the tiger is very slow, it
R uns as carefully as it can.

Oscar Smith (9)
Hove Junior School, Hove

Mind Control

My mind is weird and wacky,
Compared to mine, other lives are tacky.
People ask how my mind does such things,
Well, you see, mind control brings
The power to get whatever you want!

Nolah Bell (9)
Hove Junior School, Hove

Celebrating Differences

My friend Kelly makes me laugh out loud
She rides her motorbike through the crowd
Off we went to Candyland
I could taste sweets
I could taste more sweets
I could feel sand.

Evie Roberts (8)
Hove Junior School, Hove

Underwater Party

Underwater party
In an underwater city
Seaweed singing
Clams talking

Underwater party
In an underwater soft-play
Fish people working
Birthday boy running.

Nathan Fittock (9)
Hove Junior School, Hove

A Hot Swim

V ery hot
O minous
L ovely swim
C lear the lava
A wesome
N ever again
O bviously why my arm is half-burned.

Sarah Adams (10)
Hove Junior School, Hove

Skellig

Inspired by Skellig

His hair was dirty,
His fingers were crooked
His fingers were old and broken
His suit was torn and filthy.

Sofia Rezk Gobrail (10)

Hove Junior School, Hove

My Mouse Is Naughty!

My mouse is naughty,
He ate the cheese.
My mouse is naughty,
He played on the peas.

My mouse is naughty,
He teases the cat.
My mouse is naughty,
He sleeps on the doormat.

My mouse is naughty,
He nibbles my toes.
My mouse is naughty,
He turns on the hose.

The mouse is naughty,
He poos on the bed.
The mouse is naughty,
He snaps the pencil lead.

The mouse is naughty,
He chomps on newly-made bread.

The mouse is naughty,
He pulls hairs from my head.

The mouse is naughty,
He squeaks all night.
The mouse is naughty,
What a mite.

The mouse is naughty,
He chews the wires.
The mouse is naughty,
He makes fires.

The mouse is naughty,
He jumps in my ears.
The mouse is naughty,
He causes tears.

The mouse is naughty,
He leaves fur on the floor.
The mouse is naughty,
He scratches the door.

The mouse is naughty,
He pulls up the carpet.

The mouse is naughty,
He crawls into the trumpet.

I love my mouse!

Isabel Hankinson (8)
Hove Junior School, Hove

The Marshmallow Monster

My friends don't believe that I saw a monster,
A scary marshmallow monster.
Rick says it is not true,
Shame, it looked amazing.
How did it get eaten?
My mum didn't believe me either.
All day, I tried to think of something else,
Lollipops, eggs, raisins, no!
Lightbulbs, books, paper, no!
Oh great, it was going to be in my head all day!
Wonderful.

Marshmallow Monster is all I can think about,
Oh, I can hear a knock at the door.
"No, I'll get it Mum!" I said,
Struggling, I walked to the door.
The doorknob was just in my reach
Even though it took a bit of a while, I opened the
door and...
"Rick! It's you!" he was dressed as a marshmallow
monster!

Albert East (9)
Hove Junior School, Hove

Zoo Mayhem: Monkey Madness

"Monkey, monkey, what are you doing?"
"Jumping on rainbows is what I'm doing!"
"Oh monkey! Oh monkey! What did you do?
You jumped on that, now I've lost a shoe!"
The monkey swung,
The monkey shrieked,
The zookeepers fell, pretty much beat.
Until...
"Monkey, monkey, did you know
That you can't jump on rainbows?"
"Monkey knows! Monkey knows!
It's just my imagination!"
"Phew, oh phew! The pet tamer's here,"
The zookeepers sighed in unison.
"What should we do when the pet keeper's gone?"
And where did the tamer go?
Or come from?
Would Monkey swoop low? High?
Or right into the sky?

Off walked the pet tamer,
The monkey shrieked,
The keepers groaned.

Ellie-Ann Vu (10)
Hove Junior School, Hove

Goblins On The Netball Court

Netballs on the pitch,
Each one scores a goal,
Then the goblins started.
Balls were getting chased
A few were falling over.
Little goblins stumbled
Little puppies stomped on and slid.

Pitch is mine,
It is on,
The puppies stumbled, same as the goblins
Catch! Shot! The puppies shoot and score!
Having lots of fun, the puppies shoot again and
score.

Goblins shot one too, it was a tiny win.
Okay, it was the puppies' turn
But in that time, the netball club had begun.
Like a flash, the puppies went home,
In a mini, the goblins went too.

Now everyone got what they wanted,
Slowly, they started a party, it had just begun!

Scarlett Elise Shuff (8)

Hove Junior School, Hove

The Cat Dog And Dog Cat

On rainy days, a dog ran to a log,
That same day, a cat ran under a hat.
Then, the cat ran to the tree,
Filled up with glee,
She climbed free.
The dog ran off the log,
Climbed the fence,
Feeling the fog.
The dog was at the bottom of the swaying tree,
The cat then fell off, knee by knee.
Magic happened, lights flashed,
The dog howled, the cat crashed
They didn't know what had happened
Until they noticed their paws
And they got hot,
The cat was chewing bones
And the dog was scratching legs.
Why would this happen?
They were in shreds
Then they crashed once again, like a crime
But everyone was fine!

Emily Carolyne Teresa Catt (9)
Hove Junior School, Hove

128

My Rhyming Family

On Saturday, my cat sat on the mat
And ate a bat in a tat
But then she saw a rat which was very fat.
She put a hat on the cat and he gave her a pat
On the back.

My dad was very bad
Because he had a lily pad
And two frogs called Yad and Tad.

My mum is dumb, she always has gum
She hums, she says, "Yum, yum,"
When she has something nice.

My pet dog sits in a bog where there's fog,
He jogs every day to the log.
His name is Mog and he has friends called Zog,
Tog, Rog, Sog and Pog.

My toy train likes the rain and also chains.

Barney McQuillan (8)
Hove Junior School, Hove

Me And My Brother's Picnic

We had lots of pizza slices,
It was yummy for a very hungry tummy.
The next thing we had was an ice cream sandwich,
My brother ate it, so I had none of it.
My brother was so naughty, he ate nothing else,
So this is what I ate.
Take a good look so you know what I ate.
I ate pizza slices, ice cream sundaes
Cream buns and ice-cold slushies!

Is your brother kind of cool?
Does he always say hey?
Does he wear girly clothes?
Does he have curly hair?
Is your mum kind of weird?
Does she cook all day?

We played all day,
It was so much fun!

Tazrian Manha (8)
Hove Junior School, Hove

Magic Library

Walking in, around and around,
Nothing to hear, not a sound.
Looking, looking, where has it got to?
All I see are ones about pop. Ooh!
There it is! There it is!
Glowing in the corner,
Pull, pull, pull! Nothing's happening.
But then, there's a door.
Squeak, bang, alakazam!
Come along to Fairy Land.
Fairies flying all around,
Plenty to hear, surrounded by sound.
Mushrooms red and white, not black,
Raining sugar drops, tip tap, tip tap.
Whizzing down back to Earth, into my bed,
To flutter down and to rest my head.

Cleo Cory-Wright (8)
Hove Junior School, Hove

The Annoying Little Brother!

Nose-picker
Bogie-licker
Food-sweeper
Cry baby.
Dog-lover
Mess-maker
Troublemaker
Cupcake-kisser
Football-player
Paper-eater
Computer expert.
Hair-player
Paper aeroplane-thrower
Eye-poker
Earwax-eater
Messy-spitter
Glass-smasher
Food-thrower
Dog-walker

Cat-hater
Animal-lover
Pencil-thrower
Juice-drinker
Pie-lover
Glasses-lover
Bike-rider
Doughnut-lover
Door-slammer
Hard kicker
Weak puncher
Gum-chewer
Clothes-lover
Hat-lover.

Esme Montano-Gray (8)
Hove Junior School, Hove

Animal Poem

There are lots of animals for sale,
But who knows? It could have just been a snail.
There are rabbits with good habits,
Goats that like Coke,
Cats that like bats,
A mouse that climbed on the house.
There's a dog that likes fog,
Ducks that like trucks,
Bugs that like slugs,
Moles that like holes,
Frogs that like bogs,
Cows that like meadows,
Horses that like pauses,
Pigs that are big,
Chickens that like pickers,
Sheep that like beeps
And anything you could imagine!

Victoria Gomez (8)
Hove Junior School, Hove

Alien Invasion!

In a place far away,
A bunch of aliens decided to stay.
Whizzing through the Milky Way,
Only to find out that they had to pay!
They landed with an almighty crash,
A scream, a shout, a choke, a cough.
Out they popped, first came Bash,
Then came Bing, not forgetting little Boff.

"We've just come for ice cream!"
They exclaimed with glee.
"A chocolate fudge triple for him and for me."
"Well, if you're not going to kill us,
You can come for tea!"

Niamh Fairclough (9)
Hove Junior School, Hove

When An Alien Visits School

When the alien visits your school,
Please don't gasp in shock.
He may be purple with bright green spots
Or even blue with red polka-dots.

"Flip-flop-bippedy-bop!"
The alien's trying to talk to us!
It does sound strange, but we all know
He's only trying to say hello!

Oh wait! Scrap what I said,
He's seen your school photo
And he's running away!

But, don't you worry,
He didn't go far,
He's only stopped on Planet Mars!

Mae Vernon (9)
Hove Junior School, Hove

Monster Magic!

The monsters come to life
After you've seen what they call
A paradise.
Don't fret or scream,
They just want some ice cream
With chocolate sprinkles and strawberry sauce
Flavours of all kinds and cones you can gnaw.
With a green tongue and bright yellow eyes
Plus light blue skin and wrinkly thighs,
The sight will give you a shock
And surely a surprise.
But at the end of the day
You will want to say,
"Goodbye, Mr Monster!
I hope you enjoyed your stay!"

Lucy Grim (8) & Esme Dawson (8)
Hove Junior School, Hove

The Mythical Forest

Flowers glowing in the darkness,
Magical fairies dancing in the moonlight,
Leaves jumping really high,
It must be midnight in the mythical forest.
Moonlight started to fade,
Dawn began to break,
Furry foxes and fluffy owls went away,
It must be sunlight in the mythical forest.
Moss on the trees starting to glow,
Sunlight disappearing in the sky,
Moonlight emerging in the sky,
It must be dusk in the mythical forest.
Time to say goodbye to the mythical, magical
forest.

Florence Ross (8)

Hove Junior School, Hove

In Outer Space

In and out of space,
Naughty aliens kicked off a football match in space
One little alien cried, "Football is ace in space!"

Up in space, Harry Alien Potter was duelling
With Lord Alienmort over which team was better.
"Duel!" cried a mule.

Trouble began to hit space,
A mule got hit in the face.

"Oh no!" cried Mr Prime Minister Alien
And he rhymed to travel back in time.
"End!" cried the mule and it ended.

Sam Sutton (9)
Hove Junior School, Hove

Llama Stampede!

Llama stampede, run for your life!
Llamas are the new killing craze
And watch out for their bites.
Maybe you'll get one or two in the head
And, of course, you'll get a blood bath.

"Save us!" a person cried.
There goes Seb, there goes Josh,
At least I'm still here.
Messages are sent to the army
Pee! Watch out for their acidic pee!
Engineering a world of destruction,
Driving out the human race,
Ending this world.

Robbie Spink (9)
Hove Junior School, Hove

The Fight

The feud filled the air,
First, they flicked their hair,
Their wings were flapping angrily,
And they were all bickering viciously.

The devil stomped his feet,
His anger was all in one piece,
It was about to shatter out,
And spin like a roundabout!

"Stop! Stop!" I began to shout.
"Fairies, you can have your forests,
And Devil, the underworld."
It was a good change.

Indi Rose Gregory-Dickson (8)
Hove Junior School, Hove

My Favourite Things Are Animals

I like zebras because I like stripes
And I can see them with my eyes.

I like giraffes because they're cheeky
And I see them a bit spotty.

I like leopards because they're beautiful
And I can see that they're colourful.

I like tigers because they are neon
And they are like a lion.

I like lions because they roar
And I can roar, *rooaarrr*.

Abbey Sophie Blunsum (9)
Hove Junior School, Hove

Unicorn Dolphin

When I was a dolphin, I used to swim in the sea,
I was so quick, no one could see me.
I thought it was a dream and I was in bed,
I woke up and it was real and wasn't in my head
And all I wanted to do was steal Rainbow Drops
From the local shops.
They tasted so nice, they tasted so sweet,
The only trouble was all I wanted to do
Was eat, eat, eat!
Now I'm a rainbow unicorn dolphin!

Imogen Allen-Goble (9)
Hove Junior School, Hove

I Could...

I could hear flowers singing
And the buzz, buzz, buzzing
Of the bees at work.
I could smell the dew drops
Drip, drip, dripping off the wet grass.
I could see fields of wheat,
Gently whooshing in the wind.
I could touch the weary windows of my house,
I could step on the leafy, green grass in my garden.

I can do anything as long as I persevere
And have a great imagination

Biba Mariann Greenhouse (8)
Hove Junior School, Hove

Silly Stanley

Helps his friends
Makes you tense
Makes a mess
Brings a guest
Takes your pen
Reads the text
Meets any friend
Has one gender
Makes you surrender
Makes you a pie
Draws you a line
Makes you lie
Makes you cry
Makes you bright
Makes you write
Makes the light
Makes a sight
Has some might
Lifts you up high
And he says bye.

Armaan Reza Meah (8)
Hove Junior School, Hove

Puppy And Unicorn

My puppy went on a walk one day,
He met a unicorn who said, "Do you want to play?"
They played, running and drumming,
Then they ate plums, which were hot from the sun
And they rode a pony,
Who was owned by Tony.
They got cupcakes,
But instead, they got rakes.
They went to a campsite, but it wasn't right,
Then it was midnight and they said goodnight.

Bronte Snell (8)
Hove Junior School, Hove

Candy Alien

On my way to the moon,
Seeing stars and goo too,
I landed and stepped in a clue.
Footsteps like mine and yours.
I walked forwards and there you were,
Ow! What was that? Just an alien.
I hoped so.
They took my hand and dragged me to the floor,
Then I saw a shop that was a candy store!
I went in, I saw a lollipop
While they traded me a gummy drop.

Akisha Miah (8)
Hove Junior School, Hove

Super Evil Pizza

World-smasher
Nose-picker
Child-thrower
Balloon-popper
Finger-biter
Money-stealer
Lollipop-licker
Eye-poker
Electric guitar-player
Town-crusher
Book-ripper
Champion-shouter
Rabbit-hunter
Beatbox-player
Arm-gripper
Bone-snapper
Mess-maker
Kindness-killer
Trouble-spreader
Motorcycle-rider.

Matilda Weatherall (8)
Hove Junior School, Hove

Funny Things About My Cat

My cat is small and fluffy and fairly chubby,
My cat likes to sleep all day
And eat fish out of a tray.
My cat loves to play all day.

My cat is sometimes cheeky
And also loves to play Peaky.
My cat is scared of the roads
But is not scared of toads.

I love to play with her,
But then I get covered in fur!

Poppy Maynard Rooks (8)
Hove Junior School, Hove

Mad World

I went downstairs and the floor changed colour,
I went out on the street and the houses were
upside down,
I went in the car and it was double the size,
I went into town and the church started to shrink,
I looked at the sea and it was purple,
I blinked my eyes and I was lying in bed,
It was just a mad dream about a mad world!

Elijah Frier (8)
Hove Junior School, Hove

Snow!

Finger-froster
Frost-freezer
Magic-bringer
Drift-maker
Children-chiller
Sun-hider
School-closer
Chaos-causer
Travel-disrupter
Hand-number
Sun-taker
Dream-maker
Tongue-tingler
Fire-icer
Temperature killer
Fever-spreader
Breath-taker
Time-twister
Animal-hunter.

Luca Forsyth (8)
Hove Junior School, Hove

Disco Panda

Disco Panda likes to sing,
I think he wears things that are quite bling.
Sometimes he messes it up,
But he doesn't care at all!
Can you dance like Panda in a hall?
Panda is great and amazing,
Not always, but he does a good job.
Don't judge Panda, he is not a crime,
And his favourite colour is lime.

Etta Moxon (8)

Hove Junior School, Hove

How To Be Safe

Being safe is so important,
Excellent work, you've listened well,
Intelligent boys and girls,
Now you should be happy,
Go and enjoy your day today.

Safety is fun, but you *must* listen,
And I know you can do it if you try your best,
Fun, fun, yippee wow.
Everyone is safe, hooray!

Kaci Maria Cooper (9)
Hove Junior School, Hove

Do I Have To Go To School?

"Mum, do I have to go to school?"
"Craig, you're being a stubborn mule!
Come on Craig, it's not like the children hate you."
"They do! And the staff too!
Why can't I just stay in bed?"
"Okay son, I've got a good reason...
You're the head!"

Larnii Corrass (9)
Hove Junior School, Hove

At The Zoo

At the zoo, we went to see
Five little hamsters
That looked at me.

At the zoo, we went to see
Seven pecky penguins
That looked at me.

At the zoo, we went to see
Two lions that looked at me.

At the zoo, we went to see
Six slithering snakes
That looked at me.

Jess Baker (8)
Hove Junior School, Hove

Savage Stan

Pop a balloon on the moon
Trip up your groom
Who was a buffoon
Watching a cartoon
With a mess in his room
And who flew a magic broom
Which made a big boom
And hatched a cocoon
And drew with maroon.
Zip, zap, zoom,
He choked on a spoon.
Oh no, now I'm doomed!

Arian Vakili (8)
Hove Junior School, Hove

Candy Land!

Candy Land has the sweetest lollipops
of many colours,
Candy Land has the hardest jawbreakers
with the nicest taste,
Candy Land has volcanoes of chocolate
that squirt all over the land,
Candy Land has the mintiest candy canes,
mintier than mint Tic Tacs,
Candy Land has it all!

William James Chamberlain (8)
Hove Junior School, Hove

Shop Animals

Shop-smasher
Food-licker
Tongue-biter
Can-opener
Mushroom monster
Chaos-bringer
Fizzy-drinker
Sweet-creeper
Mess-maker
Finger-biter
Nail-picker
Germ-spreader
Shelf-scratcher
Food-muncher
Lunch-screamer
Trouble-bringer
Lolly-licker.

Lola Lemée (8)
Hove Junior School, Hove

Aliens At The Beach

I went to the beach this afternoon
To buy a big balloon,
Could you believe there was an Australian alien
Selling them for five buckaroos?
I looked around and, to my surprise,
There were aliens in disguise!
My eyes dropped out of my head
And I ran and hid under my bed!

Leo Maxwell Locke (9)
Hove Junior School, Hove

Talking And Flying Cats, How Nice!

Talking and flying cats, how nice!
They fly and talk to you happily
In-between their purrs.
They sleep in trees or even clouds
And, did you know that they do bows?
They never get old and they will never die,
They look normal, but they are real spies!

Christian Carsane (9)
Hove Junior School, Hove

Children

Nose-picker
Pet-lover
Book-reader
Picky-eater
School-hater
Lip-reader
Parent-kisser
Telly-lover
Teddy-cuddler
Sweet-lover
Chaos-bringer
Troublemakers
Lolly-licker.

Juliette Monica Long (9)
Hove Junior School, Hove

Underwater City

The city was fun,
The city was good,
The city was amazing,
The city was epic.

There were mermaids,
There was seaweed,
There were big fish,
There were small fish.

Ada Kara (9)
Hove Junior School, Hove

My Big Angry Space Dino

Food-gobbler
Drink-slurper
Brain-squeezer
King-pranker
Heart-beater
Space-lander
Big smasher
Children-frightener
Great cooker
Fast runner.

Harry Frederick Boyce (8)

Hove Junior School, Hove

Land Of Candy

Flo carefully opened her cool pencil case
Inside, she saw some sort of candy place
With a cookie for a sun,
A candy cane tree,
It was so tasty!
Oh, what an extraordinary place,
All of a sudden, she saw a face,
But luckily, it was only her friend Grace.
She said to Flo, "I've got a treat."
It was a light blue bird,
It always went *tweet!*
The bird called Bella took me to her nest,
Just then, Flo realised she was the guest.
She tried to do her best
To stare and see if Bella's eggs would hatch,
It was only one in a whole batch.
Then Flo said, "I have to leave."
Grace said, "Take this golden leaf."
Flo dreamed that night about another adventure
with Grace.

Abigail May Wallace (7)
Our Lady Of Sion Junior School, Worthing

Funderland

I opened my soft pencil case
I saw an amazing world
There were bees who were having a race!
Oh, what a beautiful place!
The bees were big, the bees were strong,
The bees liked to party all day long.
I had a dip in the river,
It was the best place ever!
I ate some of the candy,
It was scrumptious and dandy!
Afterwards, we went to a snow park
Where we had a race in the dark.
After a rest, we went to a fairground,
Lights and excitement all around.
Eating candyfloss and going on rides,
We couldn't have had more fun if we'd tried
Time to go home, say goodbye to the bees,
"Oh, can I come back again one day? Please?"

Rose Lambie (7)
Our Lady Of Sion Junior School, Worthing

Oi, Year 3!

Abigail must sit on a lion's tail
Jack must sit on a cat's back
Ethan Rowe must sit down below
Rose must sit on someone's toes
Lola must sit on a tombola
Miles must sit on bathroom tiles
Amelie must sit down carefully
Harry Mayhew must sit on you know who
Daisy must sit on something crazy
Ruebens must sit on humans
And Mia, Mia and Miya must sit on the pier
showing no fear
And Isaac Coren may sit wherever he likes!

Isaac David Coren (8)
Our Lady Of Sion Junior School, Worthing

The Ocean Filled With Drama... Caused By A Shark

I carefully opened my rainbow narwhal
pencil case
I saw an ocean filled with all the animals
from the depths
I smelled lemonade
I had to run at a pace
To get a place
For the swimming race.
I saw a colourful shark
Reading in the dark,
I found a fish walking upside down,
It looked a little like a clown.
There was a smooth whale sunbathing on
top of a snail
A glittery narwhal was flying but he was crying.

Mia Louise Gokool (7)
Our Lady Of Sion Junior School, Worthing

Crystal Wonderland

I opened my cherry juice pencil case
And poked my finger in the case
And... *whoosh!*
I got sucked in and ended up
In a land of crystal and gems.
I saw a pond that shone brightly
Like a diamond.
I met a girl and she was called Grace,
She had a dog called Ace.
I played chase with Ace,
But Ace won the game of chase.
Then we had a race
And I won the race.

Miya Croft (7)
Our Lady Of Sion Junior School, Worthing

TARDIS Pencil Case

I carefully opened my pencil case
The one that had a face,
It smelled like Sweetie Land
And I glanced inside.
I tried a bit of a tree,
It tasted of liquorice,
It was yummy!
I saw a chocolate river, it was white chocolate.
It was also snowing sugar,
I caught some on my tongue,
It made me feel so young.
I travelled one mile west
And I saw a nest.

Lola May Mortiboys (7)
Our Lady Of Sion Junior School, Worthing

What Is Inside My Pencil Case

One day, I came to school,
I put my hand in my pencil case,
I got sucked in.
It was like a race,
I tried to get out, but it was too strong.
I went down, down,
It was a wonderful place.
I saw a theme park,
The waltzers were ace,
When I got off, I fell into a secret base,
The base was ace, but I hurt my face!

Jack Isaac Seggery (7)
Our Lady Of Sion Junior School, Worthing

The Magical Pencil Case

My pencil case is a magical case
It's magical because it looks small
But really, it's a huge, great hall
With huge, great walls.
As I look about, I see some pools
Just like crystals with whirlpools
Like balls that are tall like big walls.

Amelie Victoria Chapman (7)
Our Lady Of Sion Junior School, Worthing

Becoming A Were-Dragon

I am the purple were-dragon,
I set my flight at night,
When light comes from the bright sun,
I return to a normal life.

I am the purple were-dragon,
Flying in the sky,
High above the candy clouds,
I roar when I go by.

I am the purple were-dragon
Swooping all around,
Swallowing all the rainbows
And burning up the ground.

I am the purple were-dragon,
Returning to my cave,
I never know what I do
Or if I am brave.

I am the purple were-dragon,
Back to a normal girl,

If I want to be a dragon,
I have to do a twirl.

Skye Pooley (10)
Shinewater Primary School, Langney

The Story Walker

I am the story walker,
In your books I'm found,
I mess with all the details
And change the plots around.

The mouse in The Gruffalo got eaten,
Goldilocks ate the three bears,
Cinderella's shoe was a welly
And Rapunzel didn't cut her hair.

The Wimpy Kid was courageous,
Harry Potter didn't have a scar,
Alex Rider was a bit of a coward
And Frodo got there in a car.

I am the story walker,
In your books I play,
I alter all the characters
So the endings aren't okay!

Abdurahman Halimah (10)
Shinewater Primary School, Langney

The Day I Climb The Beanstalk

The day I climbed the beanstalk,
It really wasn't fun,
It wasn't the story my mum read
When I was one.

I didn't meet a giant
Or a golden goose,
The story my mum had read
Was nowhere near the truth.

When I got to the top of that giant plant,
I saw furry feet.
It wasn't the boots of an awesome giant,
It was the hooves of a boring sheep.

There was no giant palace,
All there was were farming sheds
And all I got were some chickens
And a load of rotten eggs.

Dominic Lewis Laureles (10)
Shinewater Primary School, Langney

The Teacher Who Was A Dog

Yesterday, the weirdest thing happened to my
class:
My supply teacher was a dog!
He barked, he shook and licked all of us
And he didn't even say good morning to any of us!

He had glasses, a funky tail and even a tie!
And he said we might make a little pie.
We did a lot of maths
And we did a lot of that,
We played on the computer screens
And looked at all our dreams.

We all got badges
And we ate some cabbages.
Well, I guess this is the end,
Goodbye, my friend!

Lewis Nicol (10)
Shinewater Primary School, Langney

The Lego Land

Under my bed at 4am,
I'm in my Lego game.
I see a sign that says
It's free to play.
I speak to a child who is only three,
He has a wiry, yellow beard
And holds a golden key.
I ask him what the key is for,
He replies, "I'm only three!"
I see dirty fleas
That jump out of his tea.
Under my bed at 5am,
It's time to escape my Lego game,
It's time to leave this fantasy world,
Get up, get dressed
And go to school.

Dinh Phu Binh Andrew Tran (10)
Shinewater Primary School, Langney

The Food Girl

I am the food girl
And that is me,
My body is a real treat,
I am made of things to eat
And sometimes, I'm super sweet!

My brain is made of fizzy pop,
My hair is candyfloss,
My lips are bright red gummy sweets,
My legs are french baguettes,
My eyes are coloured gobstoppers,
I have a heart of strawberry jam,
My body is a bun.

My feet are slabs of fudge overall,
I think you'll agree,
I'm a delicious girl to eat!

Lillia-Mae McClarence-Hart (10)
Shinewater Primary School, Langney

Never Look Under Your Bed!

Never look under your bed,
It will really mess up your head.
Little people dancing around
And you will never hear a sound!

Never look under your bed,
You'll see the old books you've read
Have broken free
And are having cups of tea.

Never look under your bed,
You might bump your head,
You will find a world of magical wonder,
With monsters and nightmarish thunder!

Lacey Julie Palmer (11)
Shinewater Primary School, Langney

Surfing On A Rainbow

I am the rainbow surfer,
I fly across the sea.
Sometimes I strike lightning
And that sets my colours free.

I am the rainbow surfer,
I glide over the land.
I tickle silver clouds
And tickle the golden sand.

I am the rainbow surfer,
I get hit with gusts of air.
I tread on my hurdles of lightning
And colour the sky with flair.

Elektra Sabattini (10)
Shinewater Primary School, Langney

Riding A Dragonfly

I am the most sporty, naughty person you'll ever
meet,
For I ride magnificent creatures
That are naughty and sporty
Just like me.

They hover around
Above the ground,
Sporty and naughty you see!

Their first name is Dragon,
Second is Fly
And it's as fast as me
Like lightning going by.

I ride dragonflies!

Marissa Ansah (11)
Shinewater Primary School, Langney

Little Miss Riding Hood

Walking in the woods one day,
I met Miss Riding Hood,
She wasn't the lovely girl
From the books I'd read.

Her ears were long and pointy,
Her mouth was cruel and wide,
Her teeth were bright and full of dye.

She altered a bit with a bit of fun,
Then threw a piece of gum,
It flew right past me
Like I was dumb.

Luca Buckland (11)
Shinewater Primary School, Langney

The Bird In My Brain

The bird in my brain
Pulls my thoughts here and there,
It distracts me from my maths
And takes me elsewhere.

The bird in my brain
Chirps, flutters and hops,
When I'm doing my English,
Into my ear it pops!

The bird in my brain
Makes nests out of thoughts,
It scrambles ideas
And turns plans into naughts.

Amy Batchelor (10)
Shinewater Primary School, Langney

The Fox That Sung

I saw a fox sitting on a street,
It was singing quite a groovy beat.
It started clapping with its feet,
Then it stopped and glared at me.
I smiled and grinned with utter glee,
But then the fox ran away from me.
This experience had really made my day,
I wished the fox had stayed to play.
I love our wildlife in every way.

Louise Perkins (10)
Shinewater Primary School, Langney

Fredrik Simons

Fredrik Simons was a very wacky man,
he loved nothing more than eating pizza
whilst flying to Japan.
He was an old shaggy man,
with a lamp post as a wife.
He chose this lamp post
because he didn't want any strife.

Fredrik Simons was a very savage man,
he liked to think whilst flying to Japan.
He would think all day until he started to scratch
and bite, wow, what a sight!

Fredrik Simons was a very loud man,
he loved nothing more than
shouting out the word '*Japan*'
while doing a handstand.

Poor Fredrik Simons,
he was a very selfish man.
Nothing pleased him except for apple pie
which he could never find whilst in the sky.

Jasmin Barrow (9)
St Thomas A Becket Catholic Primary School, Eastbourne

A Further Galaxy

The grand setting of the moon
Captures the details like a spoon
The moon with craters galore
Many inches to happily explore
The moon with craters deep
Looking down, they seem fairly steep.

But, hold on, what's that shape?
Both its eyes and teeth are agape
Now this thing
Oh, what does it bring?
It seems like a box
Poking out of the top is a talking fox
The thing speaks surely
However, it seems it brushes poorly
It communicates with shrills and shrieks
Something you may hear from her multiple beaks.

It holds a brush
Sadly, it's covered in gooey mush
Yet again, it speaks
Boy, its breath reeks

I think it wants me to brush its teeth
Seemingly, they look like a coral reef
I decide;

I will,
Boy, brushing its teeth is like working in a mill
Now that's done
I can have some more fun
This was a good day
But it's always good to come back and pray
Now that this poem is done
You can sit back and watch the sinking sun.

Dominik Stasik (9)

St Thomas A Becket Catholic Primary School, Eastbourne

Magical Dream

The grandfather clock struck twelve,
My eyelids were heavy from staying up all night.
As my eyelids got heavier and heavier,
I started to feel dizzy.
I closed my eyes in the dark abyss,
I opened them after a second,
My eyelids were no longer heavy,
I was in the same room where the grandfather
clock was.

With a droopy face, I stared at the clock,
It was not what I had expected.
It was going anti-clockwise,
I tilted my head in confusion, stopped and
went outside.

In front of me was an unforgotten forest,
I walked slowly with a big smile on my face
And gazed at certain areas of the forest.
I turned to the side and found a harmless pegasus,
It had gorgeous galaxy eyes, blue, sparkling skin
And wings that were mystical.

The pegasus jumped and neighed at me
It stared and flew away.
I woke up and realised it was just a dream.

Chloe Rubit (10)
St Thomas A Becket Catholic Primary School, Eastbourne

Flying In The Milky Way

What do you think would happen if you
Sunbathed on the sun?
Do you think you might burn your bum?
Hopefully, it won't make you scream
Like a scary dream!
We'll sunbathe for a while,
While talking, we'll laugh and smile.
Some of us are trying to find sand,
As for me, I'm trying to get a tan.
On the sun, it'll be such fun,
But honestly, I burned my bum!
Please can someone help me?
I fear that I need to pee!
Let's go over to that chocolate planet
Before my bum gets worse, damn it!
The chocolate's lovely,
Everyone's jubbly.
I'm going to dive in and probably get fat,
But who actually cares about that?
We'd better get home
Because I need to book a trip to the sun on Google
Chrome

I must say goodbye
As I take off in the sky
So, goodbye!

Zara Fear (9)
St Thomas A Becket Catholic Primary School, Eastbourne

A Candy Adventure

There were once three children
Who'd been best friends forever,
No matter where they went,
They would always stay together.
The best thing they'd ever found
Was a humongous tree high off the ground.
When they saw it,
They just couldn't ignore it.
They climbed it, it was quite high,
Almost to the blue in the sky.
As they went up the tree,
There were strange things to see:
There were monkeys with hats,
Parrots with pet cats.
As they got to the top,
There was the best ever sweet shop!
They ate all the sweets up,
Then vomited into a cup.
They ran back for more,
Until their bellies hit the floor.

They couldn't walk
They couldn't talk
It was a great adventure!

Izzy Smith (9)

St Thomas A Becket Catholic Primary School, Eastbourne

Miracles Of Wonderland

Jump on a mushroom
Let Father Christmas bring gifts
A robot that gives you whatever you want
Have a snowman as a pet.

Everyone has an immortal life
You'll get inside a show
You can speak any language you want
You can walk on a cloud
Or on a volcano.

Eat a chocolate on a crescent
Drive a submarine in the night
Tables of second-hand dreams
Water that can change your life.

Marshmallows that tell your real future
Shrink to a size of a caterpillar
You can change to whatever animal you want!

Christmas crackers with reindeer inside
Kiss a dolphin

Ride on a rainbow
This wonderland has more than what you think.

Ahana Lukose (10)
St Thomas A Becket Catholic Primary School, Eastbourne

The Asteroid That Brought Us Together

The asteroid emerged into our city,
Bringing millions of flames to the earth.
All of a sudden, I started to float up,
Up, up, up and up.
Loads of equipment surrounded me
Unexpectedly, I got sucked into a black hole.
The new world was rather unusual,
For some reason, the world was weird.
The sun was a circular orange,
The Earth was still there,
But it looked funny.
Jupiter was the largest but in this world,
It was the smallest.
The giant Jupiter spot was
The tiniest spot I'd ever seen.
The galaxy was black, grey and white,
Something was rather odd about this place
And I was about to find out what...

Melissa Sara Mathew (10)
St Thomas A Becket Catholic Primary School, Eastbourne

Random Words

Today I met a unicorn
It looked colourful, it was kind
The unicorn said to me, "Have you seen the yellow corn?"
I said, "Yes, I am not blind!
I need to go, my mum said be back at five."
So I ran home as fast as lightning
Today was the day that I jumped around
Hoping I would get a pound
No I didn't, I was so bound
Guess what? It's now Monday, I'm not at the school ground
I shout and I scream
This was my dream...
Time to smile and wave
Wondering if I like ice cream
I wonder in suspense if I will go brown
Today is the day I start to crave
Today is the day I run out of words!

Eve Machache (9)
St Thomas A Becket Catholic Primary School, Eastbourne

Ocean Adventure

Yesterday, I went on an adventure
With a dolphin in the sea.
I saw a car, a bike
And a broken key.

Towards them, we swam,
Just the dolphin and me,
Wondering whether
We'd make it. Maybe?

We got to the car
And opened the door,
I struggled inside,
Then looked at the floor.

Before my eyes
Were buckets of gold,
In that moment,
The story began to unfold.

Maybe some pirates
Crashed at sea,

Or mermaids
Were stung by a queen bee.

I said to the dolphin,
Who was looking at me,
"We're rich!
Yay! Yippee!"

Anabel Murphy (11)
St Thomas A Becket Catholic Primary School, Eastbourne

The Future

I wonder what the future could hold,
Who knows, in front of your eyes, it could unfold.
Will cheap stuff be money, cards, more care?
Will the trees repopulate to make more air?
How's the football match, is the game still alive?
Will prisoners have less chance to thrive?
Will stuff be cheaper in this generation,
Is there more than a lot of nations?
Will dinosaurs be pets?
Do games have resets?
Can movies be more than PG?
Will humans become machines?
Are our favourite songs heard?
Will we evolve? That's quite absurd.

But no, we're not sure,
Let's see when it comes.

Gareth Gagante (10)
St Thomas A Becket Catholic Primary School, Eastbourne

Video Games

I play video games
With a title of little names
Playing video games is cool
Playing Yu-Gi-Oh! I always win a tournament duel,
I can always play different modes.
If you want to play a different game
Then just ask me and that's cool.
We can play Minecraft, Fortnite too
Roblox and Splatoon.
So, what do you want to play?
I'll just get it out of my way
So we can play any video game.

What game mode do you want to play?
Getting a win is guaranteed
All I'm saying is a Victory Royale without a doubt,
Okay, let's do it now,
What do you say?

Jayden Camilleri (9)
St Thomas A Becket Catholic Primary School, Eastbourne

The House Of Chocolate Burgers

Once I was walking through the woods,
My parents said I shouldn't, but I said I could!
Everything was so gooey, dark and smelly,
I could even hear the loud rumbling of my belly.
"I'm so hungry!" I began to shout
In the hope that someone would get me out.
But then something shone really bright,
It looked like it was going to ignite!
And then I stepped closer to this shiny thing
And then I saw that it was a house of yummy things!
Chocolate and burgers to my delight,
I could stay up and eat this all night!

Hayley Francisca Adjei Flores (9)

St Thomas A Becket Catholic Primary School, Eastbourne

Dreamland Fun

Glitterfalls, a great place to be,
So mystical and magical,
Just the place for you and me.
None believe their eyes when they see.

Unicorns gliding
Showing off their mighty colours,
Fairies riding
In the light of the moon.

Finally, it's the next day.
Off to the lilypads,
Time to play.
Everyone shouts, "Hooray!"

Aw, do we have to go?
It was great fun.
I'll tell everyone I know.
See you all another time!

Erin McCabe (10)
St Thomas A Becket Catholic Primary School, Eastbourne

A Crack In The Ground

One day, I went for a walk
I took my friend so we could talk.
Then... *crack! Splat!*
The ground exploded!
I saw it all in a different mode.

I was covered in chocolate from head to foot
Even though it felt like soot.
The crack in the ground was really big
It looked like the big dig.

Underneath the ground was a chocolate river
Gladly, it wasn't someone's liver.
It flowed beneath my feet,
Even though it would take me to Crete.

Morgan Hooper (9)
St Thomas A Becket Catholic Primary School, Eastbourne

Angry Man

There once was an angry man
Who lived alone in a caravan,
His wife had left him,
So this was why he was angry.

He bought a pug,
Who, every night, gave him a hug.
He had no patience
But deep down, had a sense of humour.
Don't ask me, it's just a rumour.

One morning, while he was eating breakfast,
He heard a knock at the door,
It was his wife!
It had been a long time,
She apologised and they got back together again.

Rory Fitzgerald (9)
St Thomas A Becket Catholic Primary School, Eastbourne

Fortnite, Fortnite

Fortnite, Fortnite, why are you so good?
With Tilted Towers and Wailing Woods.
Loot Lake is a flying cake
But wouldn't it be better to try and bake?
Season six just came out
And the cube is what it's all about.

Fortnite, Fortnite, why are you the best?
Because I play you, you need a rest!
Paradise Park, you are so big
Because I like you, you hold a mark.
Dusty Divot, you are full of trees,
Because you have so much, you need some seas.

Alfie Thomas (9)
St Thomas A Becket Catholic Primary School, Eastbourne

Acrostic Wonderland

W onder is something we all do,

O ver the age of two

N ew discoveries happen every day

"D o we have information on the magnetic field of Jupiter?" I ask when I may

E veryone wants to know things

R oaring for the answers like pings

"L ots of people want the answers," I say

A nd you may do it yourself

N ew questions arise every day

D o the answers come on the same day?

Shelby Scaria Thomas (10)
St Thomas A Becket Catholic Primary School, Eastbourne

The Land Of The Candies

In the land of the candies
Found near the Andes,
There were plenty of gummy bears.
All of them ran repairs
On a monument in town
That had fallen down.
The lollipops put names on some lids,
The lolli-mums put soap on the kids,
The hundreds and thousands filled the square,
Getting a bit of fresh air.
The pink shrimps did their thing
Ringing the bell, *ding a ling ling*,
In the land of the candies,
Found near the Andes.

Pablo Haylock-Fernandez (10)
St Thomas A Becket Catholic Primary School, Eastbourne

A Unicorn Cat!

One day, I found a unicorn cat,
Just sitting in its natural habitat!
When I sat on it, he took to the sky,
Eating clouds as he continued to fly.
As I stroked him, he purred and purred,
Until I realised it was coming
From the back of its fur!
When I turned,
I saw what looked like a piece of art,
But unfortunately, it was a rainbow fart!
As we landed back down, on the grass he sat,
But just imagine a unicorn cat!

Julia Antonina Karas (11)
St Thomas A Becket Catholic Primary School, Eastbourne

The Renegade Raider

The Renegade Raider is with her friend, Skull
Ranger
Safe from danger with their cosy campfire
As cosy as can be, cosier than the eye can see
Running away from a dragon on a wagon.
The dragon shot out his flames
I jumped into the River Thames
Doubting my fame
As someone proudly claimed,
"I defeated the dragon on a wagon!"
But had they defeated the snake on a rake?

Leon Holland (10)

St Thomas A Becket Catholic Primary School, Eastbourne

Meatball Island

Meatball floor
Meatball door
Meatballs, meatballs, give me more.
Meatball stairs
Meatball chairs
Meatballs, meatballs everywhere.
I like meatballs in my bed
I'll eat meatballs until I'm dead
Meatballs, meatballs in my head
Meatballs, meatballs I shall wed
On Meatball Island, I shall live
With all the meatballs I can give.

Liam Alexander Collins-Sperring (9)

St Thomas A Becket Catholic Primary School, Eastbourne

Bathroom Brilliant!

I went to the bathroom
To be filled with shock,
That it wasn't full of water
But bubbles like rocks!
In I went, into the bath,
How smooth like glass!
Nobody noticed
That I was happy at last!
I glanced and behind,
With more absolute shock,
In the bathroom wall
Was a pair of wings
That said *out of stock.*

Annamaria Manoj (9)

St Thomas A Becket Catholic Primary School, Eastbourne

Barbecue In The Clouds

I had a barbecue in the clouds,
I heard a boom so very loud.
It came from a kilometre away.
I thought it'd just ruined my day.

All of my things fell straight down.
Everything dropped to the solid ground.
I realised I had broken my leg,
Then, woke up and fell out of my bed!

Syntyche Juvan Obra (9)
St Thomas A Becket Catholic Primary School, Eastbourne

The Food Party

Silly sausages dance around,
Sweet strawberries glance around
Happy potatoes swing around
Angry lettuces shout and stamp
Creepy pizza stares you out
Lovely marshmallows hug you.

Jess Wren (9)
St Thomas A Becket Catholic Primary School, Eastbourne

Why Can't Maltesers Fly?
(A haiku)

Maltesers can't fly
But they are a light chocolate
So I don't know why.

Daniel Evans (9)
St Thomas A Becket Catholic Primary School, Eastbourne

Animal Hybrids

The penguitten stared and dove underwater,
I stood and glared as it skimmed the water.
The elefly snorted and flapped his wings,
I stumbled forwards to grab a glimpse.
The birf flicked its tail and sniffed the air,
I hurried back to avoid a glare.
The beth roared and spun around,
I tried to ignore it by rubbing my hands.
The hybrids eventually ran away
And I had time to watch them all day.

Liberty Kemp (10)
Telscombe Cliffs Primary School, Telscombe Cliffs

Drive A Submarine Round The Shop

What's that sound I hear? *Crack!*
There it goes again! *Whack!*
It's coming closer, closer still,
It's like something big is following me,
Could it be a bee I see?
No! It's a blinding, yellow submarine,
I see Sainsbury's hiding behind the icicles.
Cold, it's cooler than an iceberg
A white, furry polar bear is riding up the aisle.
Smack! Silly bear reversed back,
Have another try next time!
"Wait yellow submarine!" said Ted.
"I need to hitch a ride,
If you would be so kind,
Take me home to my icy throne."

Teddie Rand (8)
The Gatwick School, Crawley

Peter, Bob & The Chocolate Lava

Peter and Bob are best of friends,
They share everything, even pens.
One day, they find themselves in a garden,
Guess which one, the king's garden!

A great volcano sits in the middle of it,
Spouting out lava and lots of grit.
The king comes out and tells them,
"Jump in boys and you'll find a gem!"

Bob is silly, but Peter is smart,
He says to him, "Please have a change of heart."
But Bob insists, "Look at me, I'm smart.
I'll jump in using moves of martial arts!"

He throws in first his whole chocolate bar
And feels deep within that he's a true star.
But chemicals react, turning the lava
Into mighty, fantastic, delicious chocolate lava!

All of a sudden the volcano explodes,
Sending chocolate in the air and filling the roads.
The king shouts, "We are rich!
This really was a fortunate glitch!"

Edward Ramyar-Gulienetti (7)

The Gatwick School, Crawley

Chocolate Bath

Usually, I don't like a bath,
I just want to play and laugh.
When Mum called me for a bath one day,
I didn't know what to say.
When I looked inside the door,
I couldn't believe what I saw:
A yummy-looking chocolate bath!
It looked so yummy, I couldn't resist a drink,
It was like I saw my bath toys wink!
When I got in, I felt so relaxed,
My body was covered to the max.
My rubber ducky had turned chocolate too
So I had a bite.
It tasted really light,
I would never want to get out of here,
I think I'll sleep in here tonight!

Amaiyah Edwards (7)
The Gatwick School, Crawley

Crazy Things

I jumped into a chocolate pond,
It was very cool,
My strawberry cat
Sat on my mat,
Then I got wet with some goo.
Also, I heard a boo!
I rushed back home
But there was a gnome
So I carried on.
Also, while listening to my favourite song,
I saw a vanilla sun
And a chocolate bun,
A strawberry sheet
Which couldn't be beat.

Emily Butcher (7)
The Gatwick School, Crawley

Marvellous Meteors

It was a dark and gloomy day,
When I was feeding myself hay!
A marvellous meteor appeared,
The beard on my face cheered.

The meteor wore pink pants,
Inside its pants were ants.
I jumped and screamed and pretended
And that's where the glory ended.

Kayden Forder (7)
The Gatwick School, Crawley

The World!

The world was spinning around,
Then the world turned into a pearl!
The girl picked up the pearl
And swallowed it in a gulp,
The pearl was rolling around,
Then it hit the spine.
Then, suddenly...
The pearl came out and it spit!

Aisha Khan (7)
The Gatwick School, Crawley

YoungWriters®
Est. 1991

YOUNG WRITERS
INFORMATION

We hope you have enjoyed reading this book – and
that you will continue to in the coming years.

If you're a young writer who enjoys reading and creative
writing, or the parent of an enthusiastic poet or story writer,
do visit our website **www.youngwriters.co.uk**. Here you
will find free competitions, workshops and games, as well
as recommended reads, a poetry glossary and our blog.
There's lots to keep budding writers motivated to write!

If you would like to order further copies of this book,
or any of our other titles, then please give us
a call or visit **www.youngwriters.co.uk**.

Young Writers
Remus House
Coltsfoot Drive
Peterborough
PE2 9BF
(01733) 890066
info@youngwriters.co.uk

Join in the conversation!
Tips, news, giveaways and much more!

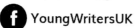 YoungWritersUK    @YoungWritersCW